For Ella,
    a chip off the old block

From Dartmoor to the Arctic Circle

CORNERSTONES

SUBTERRANEAN WRITINGS

Edited by
MARK SMALLEY

Little Toller Books

Published by Little Toller Books in 2018
Lower Dairy, Toller Fratrum, Dorset

This collection © Little Toller Books

Contributions selected and edited by Mark Smalley

All essays were originally commissioned and broadcast on BBC Radio 3 and are used here
under licence © BBC with the exception of: 'Introduction' by Mark Smalley, 'My Rock' by Tim
Dee, 'Meteorite' by Diane Johnson and 'Shale' by Neil Ansell, all of which are © the Authors,
and 'Flint' by Alan Garner' which is © Alan Garner 2017

Jacket artwork © Rodney Harris 2018

Frontis © Clifford Harper and Common Ground 2018

Typeset by Little Toller Books

Printed by TJ International, Cornwall, Padstow

All papers used by Little Toller Books are natural, recyclable products made from
wood grown in sustainable, well-managed forests

A catalogue record for this book is available from the British Library

ISBN 978-1-908213-63-1

01

Contents

Introduction

BRISTOL

Mark Smalley

Peel back the skin of the earth, scrape away the topsoil supporting its flora and fauna, and the land's skeletal substructure is revealed. As surface dwellers, we may be largely unaware of the rocks beneath our feet, but stones surely speak, despite long, obdurate silences.

This collection of essays is a conversation with substrate, arranged more or less in stratigraphic sequence from old to new. Here, a gamut of writers savour the heft and grain of rock, and how our interaction with it shapes both inner and outer landscapes. The drifts of bedrock streaked across the UK, so colourful on geological maps of the British Isles, tell of unfathomable time and movement. Picture the seismic time-lapse of multiple collisions and separations, of deserts and ice sheets giving way to tropical lagoons, and of those supercontinents Pangaea and Gondwana morphing into more recognisable landmasses. These lapidary journeys across the face of the Earth are still underway, epic tales locked into every pebble we pass. While strictly geological accounts, I feel, tend to disapprove of any sense of awe that we might feel when peering over the cliff edge of such vertiginous timescales, I'm glad to say these qualities are actively encouraged within the covers of *Cornerstones*. No mention here of tectonic subduction zones, slaty cleavage or gneissosity. Instead, William Blake's sense of seeing 'a World in a Grain of Sand And … Eternity in an hour' is reclaimed as the watchword for this field manual in which the geologically inspired imagination probes deep, into a terrain where unconformity of deep time underpins and overlays our impermanence.

Knowledge of rocks and skill in handling them has been fundamental to our survival. However detached many of us might feel from the bare rock beneath our feet, the UK's most densely populated places (except for London) still, more or less, map the coalfields and heavy industries that were dependent on minerals like iron ore. The extraction of fossil fuels casts a long and permanent shadow over the way we live, long after the last pit closed.

Rocks, however, are not just a material resource: we think and feel with them too. For W. H. Auden, his home thoughts from abroad took him back to his natal limestone country in Yorkshire. His poem 'In Praise of Limestone' evokes for me a rock as dry, bright and hollow as bone. It fast becomes a spiritual inquiry, a meditation on love, mediated perhaps by a soluble landscape. This resonates because stone is more than just elemental – even as we ingest magnesium and calcium carbonate minerals with our tea.

As above, so below. Quarrying allowed for cathedrals to be made above and below ground. Beer Quarry Caves on the Dorset coast are in a sense the inverse of Exeter Cathedral, some of whose fine limestone detailing was carved below ground at the quarry before being carted to Devon's county city. At Beer one first enters the original Roman workings, before moving through the ages, a succession of chambers having been carved out by the Anglo-Saxons, the Tudors and so on, right through to the Victorian period and the twentieth-century spaces, when the quarry closed. This is a place of wonder as much as a record of utility.

Although buildings reveal the local bedrock much less so now, in the era of the breeze block and global supply chains, vernacular buildings, in the village, town and city, still tell a story about local geology and social history. Today, the basic ingredient in cement and concrete is sand and crushed limestone, and the plaster in the walls is composed of gypsum, a powdered version of which is used to thicken tofu. Vegans, too, are lithophagous. Less visible, but even more ubiquitous, is the crushed rock from the UK's remaining quarries, sunk into asphalt as aggregate.

In his book, *The Hidden Landscape,* Richard Fortey notes that the UK's varied geology represents 'much-in-little', stitched together from more than one hundred different rock types. Some proved more of a draw than others. It was tin that put the British Isles on the map for the ancient Phoenicians, and lead production was promptly stepped up after the Roman occupation. By the time of the early part of the Industrial Revolution, the British Isles were producing half the world's output of base metals.

Besides sea cliffs and coasts, where the land runs out, and the uplands, where the landscape's ribs are revealed, where do we bump into actual geology in our daily lives? In old buildings, as well as railway cuttings and motorways. We find thin, polished veneers in our shopping malls and old banks (before we abandoned them and went online). Virtual realities are also rooted in the earth – silicon chips are made from quartzite, which has been purified by the geological processes of heat and pressure. Aspiring consumers can buy, at a click, stone for kitchen worktops and patio flagstones. These are imported, mostly. Their patient tectonic drifts across oceans have been fast-forwarded by vast container ships, while glossy websites and brochures advertising these polished granites and sandstones stay quiet about the conditions of people working inside the quarries of India and China.

★

For me, it all began with a stone. I know that I was younger than six, during my own Precambrian era, when I was told that fossils could be found in flint. I remember raining hammer blows down on a big flint nodule, sat in the backyard in a time before safety goggles, gripped by the stone held between my legs. Striking sparks, peppering the air with sharps and that tell-tale smell like cordite, I didn't find a fossil, but I remember that moment, the Promethean smell that promised fire. I caught the scent of this memory recently when going down Grimes Graves near Thetford in Suffolk. These flint workings, that were once composed of dozens of vertical shafts pockmarking the heath, were active for hundreds of years in Neolithic times, prized for the tools that were fashioned from the high-grade flint 12 metres below the surface. In some of the shafts that have been opened up, picks made of red-deer antlers, maybe 4,500 years ago, have been found in situ. This was about the same time that the first standing stones were being erected at Stonehenge, Avebury and Stanton Drew, and when Silbury Hill was being built. What no one has been able to explain is how those miners knew that the best-quality flint was present at depth in this place.

Besides their palpable utility, stones fuel the imagination. As a child, I loved the suggestion in C. S. Lewis's Narnia books that, deep underground, gemstones are still luscious and edible, ripe for the picking, compared to the 'cold, dead treasures' wrested from our shallow mines. Rocks are also shapeshifters that morph between states of being at the uncertain edges of our dreams. They can defy the Linnaean fixity implied by the old parlour game of Animal, Vegetable, Mineral. It's not just in Ovid's *Metamorphoses* that carved statues spring to life, or indeed that people are turned to stone, inert and arrested. It is said that the megalithic Rollright Stones near the village of Long Compton, on the borders of Oxfordshire and Warwickshire, represent a petrified king and his army. In William Stukeley's seventeenth-century engraving of the Rollrights, some of the stones resemble the silhouettes of people. Indeed, it is said that at midnight the stones come alive and slip down to the river to drink; the price for witnessing this is said to be madness. Another name for Stonehenge is the Giant's Dance.

Walking the seafloor between Tresco and Bryher in the Isles of Scilly at low spring tide, I have followed walls dating back to Neolithic times; fringed with bladderwrack, they are more wet stone than dry stone. It is extraordinary that the walls confirm that this drowned landscape was once composed of fields, and that the islands today are just the archipelago's highest ground. As recently as the end of the last Ice Age it was probably a single landmass. If we are alert to them, we can experience many such juxtapositions, such as that between inert rock and high-speed steel, when the train pulls into Liverpool's Lime Street Station. The line passes through a deep cutting hewn from the living rock, with spectacular soot- and smut-blackened Old Red Sandstone bearing the fronds of hardy ferns. Carbon meets the Pre-Carboniferous.

Pebbles encountered on walks and on beaches gather on windowsills and surfaces in my home until finally their time is done, or their origin is forgotten, and they're relegated to the front garden. Here they lurk in furtive conversation, a babel of different dialects. There are pebbles as brown and lumpen as old spuds, the inevitable heart-shaped ones, those with holes in, and many kinds of speckled granite. Peculiar but very pleasing iron-veined mudstone structures from the Cleddau estuary, Pembrokeshire, struggle to comprehend an exquisitely symmetrical black basalt teardrop from Iceland.

None of these stones is as striking as the veined green and red serpentine pebbles from the beach right outside the youth hostel at Coverack on the Lizard, which speak of the Moho Discontinuity, evidence of that margin where the Earth's crust meets the mantle 7 kilometres below the surface. Keep digging and you'll come to Australia, I was told, where everything is upside down, and

Christmas dinner is eaten on the beach. Such early encounters with Earth stories turned the more credible into the surely preposterous: shiny black Whitby jet was in fact fossilised monkey puzzle tree.

Clearly, when it comes to rocks, anything goes. Such distinct mineral journeys, marked by their elemental encounters with fire, water, desert, ice and endless time, are inscribed in the pebbles around my home. The best of the beauties that emerge from my stone tumbler, unprepossessing pebbles now shining like gemstones, take pride of place in my pocket, until they, too, get lost.

The great storyteller Hugh Lupton is a descendant of Arthur Ransome, the author famed for setting *Swallows and Amazons* in the Lake District. Less well known is that Ransome witnessed the Russian Revolution, first-hand. In a performance entitled *The Homing Stone*, Hugh Lupton tells the story of his great-uncle's flight from Moscow to the Baltic coast with his lover, Evgenia Petrovna Shelepina, Trotsky's former secretary and Ransome's future wife. In the writer's pocket throughout this journey was his talisman, a Lakeland stone, that linked him to home.

Our relationship with stone can be deeply personal, however unyielding and unforgiving the rock is. My broken roots are sunk into Northamptonshire ironstone. I recall the wonder of its warm, rusty colours, a rock that seemed to release its own rich molasses light, contrasting the vivid summer greens of grass and the overlapping shadows of chestnut leaves. Here, the ochre sandstone walls are easily marked by people. Once I was shown, by the relative of a neighbour who had emigrated to Canada many decades before, his name scratched into the wall as a boy, a life having been lived in between. I watched him re-inscribe his name with a penknife, cutting away the lichen, digging deeper. He is now long gone but his name is still – only just – legible.

Besides dust and ashes, what remains of us when we're gone, our brief lives nudging up against deep time? Perhaps this paradox is something we want inert rock to bear witness to. Rock becomes us, before we in turn are interred. It's not just the earliest worked flint tools or graven images marked with Ogham or Linear A that make stones speak; so do gravestones and that scratched name upon the sandstone wall. Glimpsing the fossils in them, so like seashells, I had my own childhood equivalent of post-Darwinian vertigo, recognising that my home in the middle of England had been formed below the sea. And though I don't live in Northants anymore, that landscape and its geology underpins me. Many of us might have our stones of choice, that shape our favourite landscapes. And that is what is at the heart of all these essays, as they seek to unlock the tales that the rocks tell.

Rocks can be signs that are taken as wonders, their apparent permanence shifting uneasily alongside their own endless journeys through cycles of erosion, deposition and metamorphic transformation. They are unarguably material and real; you always know when you've tripped over a stumble stone, but rocks are also powerfully assertive metaphors that help us think-feel our way towards the intangible.

Lewisian Gneiss

OUTER HEBRIDES

Sara Maitland

All morning the rain had been scudding in, a grey, fine mist of rain and you cannot see the islands out there dancing on the waves. Then, suddenly, magically it all changes: the sun is shining, the air golden with its own dampness, and torn fragments of rainbow jump out unexpectedly from behind the shoulders of the hills. And you cannot but see that this is a shattered landscape – fractured, broken, deserted, beautiful.

I had turned off the main road at Ardvreck, the ruined castle on Loch Assynt, and was taking the loop of road along the north shore of the loch to Lochinver and then the tiny coastal villages of Achmelvich, Clachtoll, Clashmore, Stoer, Clashnessie, Drumbeg and Culkein. The difference between sea and land is blurred by the lochans on the land and the islands on the sea – and the whole place is dominated, when the rain lifts, by the vertical crag of Suilven to the south, which looks bizarrely more like a tourist visitor from the Arizona desert than like any Scottish mountain.

I had to keep stopping the car, too moved by the extraordinary desolate landscape to be able to proceed with the due caution that the small twisty roads called for. There is here in the Western

Highlands an overwhelming loveliness that cunningly disguises just how weird the whole place is. In summer there is a soft shining quality to the light, which goes on and on into what ought to be night-time and is not; the sea lochs reach deep into the hills with thin curving fingers like birds' claws; the birch trees gambol down vertical slopes; the sand on the beaches, which is not sand at all but ground-up seashells, is startlingly white; the small islands just off the shattered coastline perform baffling disappearing tricks as the tide rises and falls.

Between the vertical, weirdly stacked and strangely shaped mountains there are glacier-carved bowls of greenness and innumerable tiny lochans tossed down like silver coins, and tangles of rocks – every colour, every shape and making very little sense to those, like me, more used to orderly, explicable landscapes.

I drove, I walked a little on the beach and in the woods, then, wet but deeply contented, I came back eventually onto the A894 and turned north towards. . . well towards nowhere much. North of here there is Kylescu, Scourie, Kinlochbervie, Cape Wrath and the Arctic Circle. There are barely three human beings per square kilometre; the secondary school at Kinlochbervie has fewer than fifty pupils and you are nearer to the Arctic Circle than to London. Beside the road, above Loch Glencoul – a glacier-carved fjord fed by the highest waterfall in Britain, the Eas a' Chual Aluinn, and where the seals lounge on the rocks, dreaming of selkies and sexy fishermen – there was once the village of Unapool, a Viking anchorage, a crofting community; there was a tiny café (so small that it does not even run to a car park, you just pull up beside the road) boldly advertising itself as The Rock Stop Café and Exhibition Centre. So I stopped and went in. At first, it was what you might expect: Formica table-tops, home-made scones, volunteer service and beyond that a little exhibition room with a rather excellent video explaining why this is a hub of the North West Highlands

Geopark – part of a UNESCO-designated network of areas whose aim is to contribute to global understanding of geology and promote sustainable development. (There are seven in the UK.) As I went through to have a proper look, one of the café staff said: 'Could you take this with you, please? One of the children moved it, you'll see the gap on the table,' and handed me a chunk of rock, perhaps the size of a walking boot. It was very dark-coloured but shot with crystalline striations, almost sparkly. And obligingly, casually, I took it from her and strolled through.

There was a table covered with other samples of rock and indeed a gap with a label. I glanced at the label, which said 'Lewisian gneiss', and I was reeling – both in the local Scottish sense of dancing, like the little islands, and in the deeper sense of losing my bearings, my own centre of gravity, time and stability.

In my hand on a wet late morning in the middle of nowhere I was holding the oldest thing I will ever hold. Lewisian gneiss is one of the oldest rocks on the planet, about the oldest thing lying on the surface of our Earth that you can see and touch: it emerged from the mantle over 3,000 million years ago.

We have rather lost sight of just how huge one million anythings is. Think about it: there have not yet been a million days in AD time, there have not even been three-quarters of a million days – and yet that seems so very long ago. *Homo sapiens* has not been around for a quarter of one million years. Three thousand million years is unthinkable. It is almost unimaginable.

Lewisian gneiss forms the foundations of the Outer Hebrides – hence its name, Lewis, being the largest island of that archipelago. It also forms many – but bafflingly not all – the Small Isles of the Inner Hebrides, and the north-western coast of mainland Scotland. It is igneous rock formed deep in the Earth's mantle when the world was still burning hot and had no hard outer crust. While still molten, the gneiss was mixed with minerals, marbles, quartzite, granite magma and mica (hence the stripes – essentially rolled-out or ironed globs of mineral) and metamorphosed by heat and pressure. But all this happened slowly, very slowly.

Not only is it one of the oldest rocks, it is also one of the furthest travelled. The Lewisian gneiss, the bedrock of north-western Scotland, is an immigrant from very far away. It was pushed up towards the surface somewhere more than 60 degrees south – where Antarctica now is. It was certainly little comfort to the Highlanders cleared from the land I am driving through now and sent off on ships across the world to Australia and New Zealand to know they were going home, going back to where they started, but so it was.

At the time when the gneiss surfaced, there was no land at all in the northern hemisphere, it was all sea; but about 2,000 million years ago, as more of the crust became solid, the lithosphere floated on the hotter material pushing up from below it and the first of the supercontinents, Columbia or Nuna, formed. Then Columbia broke up into separate continents; came together again 1,000 million years ago as Rodinia; broke up and reassembled as Pangaea, and then split again into Laurasia – from whose substance Eurasia and North America is formed – and Gondwana, from which almost everything else was constructed.

And through all these aeons, in all this inexorable, slow violence, the Lewisian gneiss crept northwards, still part of the land mass that would eventually become North America. And ultimately, rather more than 400 million years ago, it crashed into the proto-Europe. England, also moving northwards but on a very different trajectory, was joined on to Scotland with a rough seam called the Iapetus Suture, which runs from the Solway Firth to Lindisfarne. (The Romans got it remarkably nearly right when they built Hadrian's Wall to re-divide the countries.) At this point, of course, England was still joined to Europe – that separation, which created the English Channel, happened only about half a million years ago – a relative baby in geological time.

This destabilisation, this crashing-into-each-other of continents, land masses, great plates of rock is more common than we dare to think and it changes everything. Unsurprisingly, it causes earthquakes and volcanoes, and it thrusts up mountain ranges. This process of mountain building is called orogeny, and in fact it is quite simple: put your hand firmly on your tablecloth (ideally on a smooth table but with something heavy at the far end) and push gently: you will see the at-first smooth cloth lifting into semi-parallel folds with flatter bits between them; if you keep pushing gently, some of the peaks of the fold will rise so high that they topple and collapse into the hollows between them. That is what happens, slowly, when one large mass of rock shoves against another. This particular collision caused all sorts of excitements – including the uplift of a mountain range that ran from what is now Norway right through to the Appalachians, probably higher than the Himalayas are now.

But the journey was not over. A new crack opened on the planet's surface and more molten material poured up through it. This is called the Mid-Atlantic Ridge and it began to push what is now America and Europe-and-Africa apart (you can still easily see on a map how western Africa and the east coast of South America fitted so very neatly together). This huge muscular thrust tore the Lewisian gneiss into pieces – large pieces of it are still found in Greenland and Canada (creating another unrealised homecoming for the displaced Highlanders), as well as here, in north-west Scotland and the Hebrides. Deep under what is now the Atlantic Ocean, this fresh rock is still welling up, creating new material, spreading out and pushing America further from Europe. Scotland is still moving northwards, tugging southern Britain with it.

Always travelling on, always changing, leaving cryptic messages of its long, slow passing. It moves at about the speed that fingernails grow and it is, at present, impossible to know where it may be heading.

We often speak of a multi-vehicle road crash as a 'pile-up'. This is a wonderful image for what rock masses do when they crash into each other. The cars are crushed and the folds of metal on their once-smooth surfaces rise in long crosswise folds, like mountain ranges. But they also climb up or plunge under each other; they become entangled, hard to separate. The backmost car may rise over the one in front of it, but that pressure will affect the car in front of that, which might, for example bury its front under the one in front of it. This is what happened in the western Highlands. Although the gneiss arrived first – it is the bedrock, the foundation stone – it is not always at the bottom of the stack, with the later-formed rocks laid neatly in their layers above it. It is the most ancient thing, but in places it has been pushed to the surface – along the northern shore of Loch Glencoul, for example, there is a cliff face where you can see the distinct line where the gneiss was forced up over the relatively infantile limestone. No one had to mine deep into the ground to find the piece of gneiss that I was holding in my hand in the little café; it is just lying about the countryside; sometimes in small chips like this, sometimes in low hummocky hills, now peat-covered and recognisable by the frequency of the little lochs that the glaciers have cut; sometimes in what seemed, until recently, mysterious configurations. The landscape here looks shattered and broken up because, quite literally, it is.

After these rocks were laid down, they were split and mixed up by the Moine Thrust – the first fully identified thrust fault, discovered in 1906, which provided the conclusive evidence that rocks do indeed move; their complicated, difficult stories confused by the ice ages, by the long scouring of the weather, by their struggles and dances. The geology of north-west Scotland is a mess – a glorious, savage, beautiful mess, and it was the Lewisian gneiss that started it.

The same geological history applies across the Minch, out there on the Outer Isles, but it is simpler in many ways, simpler and purer. The gneiss there is less messed about and broken; there was no Moine Thrust, no deep fjords, no grinding glaciers and confusing stratification. And on the uttermost west of Lewis, facing out towards the Atlantic with nothing beyond it except tiny, abandoned St Kilda's until you get to the Americas, some people we do not know much about for reasons we know even less about, created one of the oldest stoneworks still standing in Britain. The Callanish Stone circle is not quite as old as Steness, on Orkney, or Avebury and Stonehenge in Wiltshire, which are all now dated slightly before 3000 BC, but at between 2900 and 2600 BC, it comes close. It is a Neolithic complex of circles and avenues of stones creating a cruciform pattern and a chambered tomb with outlying secondary sites. It is, for me, one of the prettiest of all the ancient stoneworks, standing on a low ridge above Loch Roag in the beautiful, desolate landscape of sea, machair and rocky hills. When the sun is shining the pale stones seem to shine, too, to glitter even. This should come as no surprise – because the word 'gneiss' is probably derived from an Old German noun *Gneist*, meaning 'spark'. Callanish is constructed out of Lewisian gneiss – and it sparkles in the sunshine, dancing as the waves and the islands dance.

Of course, those Neolithic people, who put that extraordinary effort into building their sacred site (we still do not know quite how they did it), cannot have known that they had chosen one of the most ancient rocks in the world. They cannot have known that it had travelled almost the whole way across the globe. But they aligned their sharp-pointed rocks to the stars, and we will never know what they knew. Gneiss is deeply strange and magical.

Samiland

THE FINNMARKSVIDDA

John Burnside

On my work desk, amid a litter of pencil shavings and rubber bands, there is a grey-brown lump of igneous rock that, when occasion demands, I pick up and hold in my fist, the feel of it as weighty and reassuring as an ancient talisman. I collected this shard of time at 70 degrees north, not far from the UNESCO World Heritage site at Alta. It was September 2002, the end of the season, all the tour buses and camper vans heading southwards, leaving the stony alpine meadows empty, but for me and an old woman who had come out with a long narrow trug to gather the last of the cloudberries just south of the town. I had no reason to be there other than to saunter, alone, through the carved stones at Jiepmaluokta (a Sami word that means 'bay of seals'), trying to imagine myself into the life of the people who lived here between four and eight thousand years ago, people who built flat mazes out of stones in the open ground and carved extraordinary petroglyphs into the hardest rocks, images of hunters and animals and fishermen in long, narrow boats, herds of reindeer, each one distinct in its markings: fertility symbols and geometric patterns, human figures who seem to be dancing or playing drums, welcoming the return of, or bidding farewell to, the life-giving sun.

We know very little about the people who made these sometimes crude, sometimes rather sophisticated marks in the sandstone outcrops of the high Arctic; were it not for these two thousand or so petroglyphs, we would know nothing at all. Some of the carvings seem to function as maps of reindeer migrations and the movements of marine creatures; others have the magical power found in the marks that all hunters make, on cave walls and in chiselled stones, invoking the goodwill of the prey they depend upon. Some show groups of figures engaged in what appear to be ritual dances, agile, pagan creatures, so vivid they suggest the grace and power of Nijinsky's *The Rite of Spring*, which caused a riot when it was first performed in Paris in 1913. Did that high society audience, in their evening dress and silk gowns, catch a sudden glimpse of the pagan in themselves that night, as the great dancer leapt onto the stage? Were they frightened by what they saw? No doubt some were – but there would have been others who were thrilled by that vital energy, and by gestures and movements that recalled, not only the geographical north, but also for the most northerly point of the human psyche, a place in the mind that is both starkly wild and utterly calm.

I love the dancers and the drummers carved into the rocks. I love the sense of movement, of animal grace I get, staring at them through the scrubby heather. I love the bears – considered a sacred animal by the Sami, who say that a bear is 'as strong as twelve men, and as clever as ten.' Even more than these, however, I love the boats, with their elk-shaped bowsprits and long fishing lines, on which these sea-hunters ventured into the cold Arctic waters to catch the sacred halibut, which appears to have been the most difficult and prized of marine prey – not surprising, when a large halibut might weigh in at 300 kilos. What the carvings suggest is that this place, this bay of seals, was a meeting point between nomadic hunters from the interior and the coastal dwellers who lived on cod and coalfish, seal and haddock and halibut. They also leave the distinct impression that the people who once lived here set a high value on cooperation when it came to gaining a living – and so, a vital culture – from the land. For example, one huge carving shows men working together to drive reindeer into a corral; elsewhere, groups of hunters confront bears, or stalk elk across the stony terrain; men go to sea in groups as large as twelve, and sometimes more, working together to find the great shoals of smaller fish, or to haul in the great halibut. These people seem to have worked together, in kinship with the other creatures and, overall, I cannot help coming away from Alta with a sense of exhilaration. True, the humans in these carvings are no more than stick figures and though the animals can be powerfully drawn, the guiding principle – for good reason, given the nature of the material being carved – is economy of design. Nevertheless, what comes across most strongly is the exuberance and endurance of men and women from various kin groups meeting and working together to hunt and dance and perform the great shamanic rites that were once practised throughout the circumpolar region.

Naturally, the depictions of reindeer here are plentiful. Doubtless, their importance as a food source made them obvious subjects for the carvers, but it is clear that they are also objects of admiration, even reverence. They appear in large herds, or singly; mating, or pregnant; hugely detailed in their individual patterns, often vividly present, in spite of the simplicity of the lines, the sense of their creatureliness almost palpable. Reindeer are the source: according to one old Sami myth of origin, the Creator made this world from the beating heart of a young reindeer, around which rivers and forests were constructed from its hair and blood. If a true Sami is troubled or far from home, that myth says, he or she need only lay an ear to the ground and listen to the beating heart of this world, to find comfort and reassurance.

I once asked Harald Gaski, the Sami writer and activist, if he ever did this: his reply was that, sometimes, he was afraid to. He did not want to tempt fate; he did not want to lay his ear to the ground and hear nothing. What would it mean, I asked, if there were no sound? He said he would let me work that out for myself – and considering the damage that we self-designated civilised folk have done to sacred places and songlines around the world, not to mention the harm visited upon great herds and shoals and flocks of other creatures, I did not find it difficult to reach a conclusion.

That sense of the other creatures can still be felt here, however – and all too often, it is attended by a kind of homesickness, a nostalgia for the wild, perhaps, that resides deep in the flesh. I remember, once, meeting an Arctic fox out in the open, right at winter's end. As I neared, it stopped and, with no apparent fear, looked me over and, having sized me up, loped away, unconcerned. It had probably heard me long before I saw it – Arctic foxes have extraordinarily keen hearing – and it may well have trotted over just to take a look at this out-of-place popinjay in his blue hiking gear. Anywhere in this land of lakes and streams, pintails and other ducks call cheerfully across still bodies of icy water, while on a winter's day, flocks of perfectly camouflaged ptarmigan materialise out of the snow and explode into your path, emitting loud, disgruntled cries that, together, sound like some mad avian Geiger counter. One morning in midsummer, on a lonely strand to the west of here, I watched a family of white-tailed eagles as they soared and dived again and again, hunting for fish but also, it seemed, playing together in the warm sun. Moose live here, and where there are moose, there are wolves; though it has to be said that, for me, the most inspiring encounter that I had on the *vidda* was when a herd of reindeer crossed my path, forcing me to stop, not just because of the obstacle they presented, but for the sheer beauty of it, the sense of teeming, miraculous life. The

Sami have many words for reindeer: when Gaski was translating a poem by Nils Aslak Valkeapää which consisted entirely of such words (along with the onomatopoeic sounds of the herd and of the men who were following it), he was obliged to go to the great Northern Sami writer and musician to ask how he should proceed. Valkeapää's response was that Gaski should leave the poem as it was, to serve as a reminder to outsiders that, because they have evolved alongside the land they inhabit, only the Sami have the skills – the language, the crafts – to manage it. That language, those crafts, have developed in response to the *vidda*, just as, elsewhere, language and craft have developed through the drama of dwelling in woodland, desert or prairie.

When we learn to speak – or better, to listen – in the local idiom, when we learn to appreciate the local crafts and technologies, when we know something of the ways of the local animals and flora, we learn to find our place on the land. Is it such a surprise that, wandering into the north, armed with nothing better than crude and reductive pidgin, we damage it, sometimes beyond repair?

On the other hand, the land is no better served by those people who say that they feel tiny and insignificant when they stand out on the Finnmarksvidda, where temperatures can drop to -50°C and the wind speaks in strange tongues on a winter's night, carrying the spectre of wolverine and ice-bear through the streets of narrow settlements in its long, unremitting howl. In summer, the wide plain is beautiful, spotted with Arctic poppies and gentians, but the mosquitoes are merciless and the white nights unforgiving to anyone with sleep problems (a long-term insomniac, I have gone days in the north without sleeping, falling into hallucinatory reveries, my ears tuning into sounds no one else can hear, the ghosts of imaginary ptarmigan fluttering up from the ground at my feet). This land lives by a different clock, its timelines are close to unimaginable, so perhaps it is not surprising that people say they feel dwarfed by it all. For my own part, though, I do not share that sense of insignificance. Perhaps I lack humility, but walking out on this wide plateau – 22,000 kilometres square, or around 8,500 square miles – I am more inclined to feel like a privileged witness to a vast and mysterious fabric of place and time, a fabric of which I, in my way, am one part. True, I am not obliged by sheer, unrelenting contingency to live with anything like the grace and inventiveness of those predecessors who carved the Jiepmaluokta petroglyphs, but if that contingency comes again – and it may well do, for any number of reasons – I hope I will accept it in the same spirit, and with the same pagan vitality as they did. For now, all I can or need do is speculate as to what figures I might carve into the hard sandstone, should the occasion arise.

It is also true that I can only speculate about the lives those rock-carvers led, but I cannot imagine them feeling insignificant here, either. They performed shamanic rites that, according to their belief systems, held the community of living things and stones and ghosts together. They probably came out of their winter shelters to welcome the sun back from its dark journey on the first lit morning, as the later Sami people do in a painting by Otto Sinding that I once saw in the Nordnorsk Kunstmuseum at Tromsø, their arms raised, their faces tilted to the light, elementally dependent on this beneficent force, and elementally alive.

It seems to me that the feeling of insignificance we post-Christian people feel in the face of great natural phenomena is a hangover from the days when we thought ourselves absurdly important, God's chosen, sitting at the centre of a universe that, in our arrogance, we chose to believe was rotating eternally around us. That arrogance was a sin against nature and common sense, but then surely the sense of insignificance is just as great a sin. I have no desire to romanticise the people who followed the reindeer through these lands 8,000 years ago – that, too, would be a kind of sin – but it strikes me that one quality of pagan life, where a god or a spirit dwells in every river and every birch wood, is a sense of proportion. A sense of scale. To the pagan mind, might not everything have been just the right size? Does it not seem likely that those early hunters and fishermen – who were also singers and dancers and practitioners of many kinds of benevolent magic – does it not seem likely that those pagan people would have rejoiced in the vastness of the *vidda*, even while they felt keenly the immediacy of its perils? Some say their songs were born out of a need to calm their herds – and themselves – when the yelps of the wolf pack, or the banshee cry of the wolverine, came uncomfortably near. Some speculate that the carvings they left on these rocks were reminders of the need to work together, in the face of great danger, in order to survive. I do not think that they would have felt insignificant, as they laid their crude chisels to the stones. On the contrary, I believe they would have known themselves as privileged celebrants of a life that, while it might have seemed larger than them, also included their dreams and songs in its mysteries. That would have been the long-term lesson of living on the *vidda*: that we are neither great, nor worthless, but creatures under the sun, like the bear and the elk, the halibut and the seal, the reindeer crossing the great plain and the Arctic poppy that turns on its delicately engineered stem to follow the sun in its path through the sky.

Whinstone

NORTHUMBERLAND

Sarah Moss

Basalt and dolerite are very old and very dark. They are similar forms of igneous rock, which is a pleasing linguistic contradiction. Fire rock, flaming stone. I lived with basalt in its new, barely cold form in Iceland, where the sandy beach below our apartment was black and the lava field we crossed to reach the main road was land in the shape of waves, as if liquid had frozen in movement and then been haphazardly covered with turf and birch and rowan bushes. That was pretty much what had happened. Lava had solidified by the coast and when the sea froze after Christmas its shape reflected in blue and grey ice the white waves of snow-covered rock on land, arrested waves of water and fire and stone from one horizon to the other. Igneous rock is what bubbles up from the core of our planet, the stuff at the very centre of life on Earth which is not solid, no kind of foothold. Basalt is sometimes used for cobbles and paving stones, often crushed to make roads. When French students pulled up the pavements in 1968 they were lifting slabs of firestone. *Sous le pavé, la plage*, they said, but if you go down far enough it's not the beach but liquid mineral fire, the contradictory raw material of the world. I began this piece thinking that I should resist the urge to use geology as a metaphor, that I should try to speak of rock as rock, to respect the meanings of its mineral state without needing to make it political or poetic, but I am at it already. At the centre of everything is stone, is liquid, is flame, elements out of their element.

Liquid fire-rock seeps and bubbles below our feet, below the sewers and drains, below the underground carparks and trains, but in some places the ground beneath our feet is thin or cracked or not quite stable. Well, when you think about it that way the whole planet is not quite stable, the tectonic plates in perpetual, if normally imperceptible, motion. In Iceland, instability was plain to the naked eye. Mud simmered through the winter, steam rose from the land and we walked to school and work and nursery along paths that undulated across the lava fields. Back home, our lava is old and still, and we see the drama of its movement cold in the bones of these islands. Think of the black pillars of rock along the coast of the Isle of Skye, of the strange columns and cantilevering of Fingal's Cave, the dark slabs of the Giant's Causeway. As the names suggest, these are places where the shapes of the land seem too purposeful or maybe just too weird to be natural, places that can be explained only by the strength and strange purposes of giants, all in fact formed by the movement and gradual cooling of igneous rock forcing its way past and through the older sedimentary rock.

In Britain we find most of our basalt and dolerite in Scotland, running from just above Berwick-on-Tweed across to the Solway Firth and under the Irish Sea to Belfast, from where it continues across the border to Antrim's Atlantic coast. Igneous rock tends to attract castles and fortifications because it makes vantage points, sudden peaks and uprisings in otherwise gentle and fertile landscapes. Edinburgh Castle stands on such a volcanic mound, and the streets of the Old Town below are paved with dolerite. Lindisfarne and Dunstanburgh castles overlook the sea from the same kind of rock, visible from miles across the water and up the coast. Now of course there are roads to both of them, but last summer I insisted that we walk, approaching Lindisfarne over the mudflats the way people have done for centuries. The island seems low when you're on it, your feet on solid ground, but it's hard to climb up the banks from the tidal flats to the fields lying around the volcanic mound of the castle. We took off our boots to cross the bay – easier to wash skin than clothes before looking around an English Heritage property – and felt the seabed sucking at our feet as the castle filled half the sky above us, a literal worm's eye view of a building that has stood for centuries. I approached Bamburgh with a little more dignity, running along the coastal path, and again its bulk rose between sea and sky.

I like long-distance running partly because after a while it feels as if my body and the land I am crossing are in a conversation that only occasionally includes my conscious thoughts. When I run I like straight lines that require no effort of navigation: rivers and coasts when I can get them, canals when I'm at home in the West Midlands, long straight roads if there is nothing else. The Northumberland Coast Path is perfect – no question of which way to go when you're just following the edge of the land – but it is the volcanic outcrops punctuating it that call me to go just another mile, to run until the landmark that was on the horizon when I set off has become a tangible presence. Bamburgh seemed unreal even as I crossed the field of cows at its feet. It is a cameo of itself, the outline of a fantasy castle projected onto the sea and the sky, and even close up its scale is inhumanly large, its black stones and towering ruins plainly beyond the needs and reach of mortal man. Like Hadrian's Wall, like so many border fortifications, it is an architecture of intimidation as much as practical defence.

We walk Hadrian's Wall, all four of us. There are parts I would like to run, but not the sections which follow the bones of Whin

Sill, the local name for this swathe of old, cold lava. It's too steep, too stony, requires exactly the kind of concentration that I don't want when I run. Whin Sill juts out of the curving moorland and rising fields of the border country, breaks the pattern of contours rolling from the Yorkshire Dales to the Cheviots. I love Northumberland partly because I didn't go there as a child, so it has no familial associations for me. I choose it. I like the big skies and the big beaches and the way the moors offer you up to wind and weather. On a clear day, there is no concealment in a northern moorland landscape, nothing hidden and nowhere to hide. You know where you are. But there is also infinite detail in the blooming and withering of heather, the attentions of bees, the indentations of water-skaters' feet on the surface of a peat bog. I like to sit or lie in the heather until the birds forget I'm there, to watch the progress of caterpillars across stones and the reflections of reeds in ponds red with iron, and then to look across miles of hillside to the Roman wall. Many of the roads around here follow the characteristic ruled lines of the Roman Empire, but the wall itself curves and swoops, married not to a straight line in someone's head but to the surges of long-ago lava. You can see Hadrian's Wall from a very long way away – I have seen it from the cruising altitude of a passenger plane – and having seen it, of course, you then see Roman soldiers huddled in their cloaks, effing and blinding about the climate and the food, and maybe you see Roman centurions in their stone-built offices with underfloor heating and British boys serving them wine and olives. Maybe you see British tribespeople – let's have some woad, let's paint them blue – sneaking through the mist towards a 'milecastle' (watchtower), spears at the ready. (What you are seeing, of course, is based more on childhood readings of Rosemary Sutcliffe and Auden than historical expertise. Many of those soldiers came from northern Europe and were quite used to the cold and rain.)

Hadrian's Wall was not really a military necessity but something of a vanity project, a statement like the walls going up now around the edges of the European Union and, at least in the imaginations of many voters, along the southern border of the USA. It wasn't the edge of England because England wouldn't be invented for another few centuries. It was the edge of an empire stretching in modern terms from Syria to Scotland and from Egypt to Belgium, often following the lines of the natural features that have shaped Europe's fights for millennia: the Alps, the Rhine and the Danube. When you stand behind the wall, on the southern side because there is a precipice to the north, your imagined country doesn't end at the white cliffs of Dover but at the Nile. There are carvings of lions and crocodiles in the Roman town at Corbridge, one of the supply towns for the legions stationed along the wall, and it is perfectly plausible that the carver had seen these creatures in the flesh in North Africa.

We start one day above Vindolanda, a Roman town undergoing excavation for nearly half a century now. They've found hundreds of leather shoes in all sizes, bearing the wear of local walks on long-dead feet. (The most startling find is now in the British Museum, a series of letters to and from the families stationed here, including the first words known to be written in Britain by a woman. Claudia Severa, the wife of a Roman commander, writes to her best friend: *I miss you. The kids are doing OK. Please come to my birthday party.*) But we're not here for the town, or for the Roman footsteps and voices. It's a bright day, probably uncomfortably hot down south, but here only warm enough to coax scent from the heather and turf. It's late August and already the rowan trees along the wall are vivid with orange berries, the leaves of the oaks sheltering farm buildings beginning to turn. The kids don't want to linger over ghosts but to chase the wall across the land, over the hills and far away.

We're following the parts that survive best for the next couple of days, because where the wall crossed flat and fertile land people in the last two millennia tended to want to build houses and barns and churches and if there was a line of nicely dressed stone set out for the taking, of course they were going to take it. There are disjointed bits of Roman inscriptions and decorations in the cornerstones and lintels of cowsheds, farmhouses and bridges all through the border country, but Whin Sill undulates so steeply that the Roman soldiers (and now the National Trust) had to build runs of stone stairs to follow the wall. The children race up, casting scorn on the older people standing aghast at the bottom or pausing for breath a little way up. Enough of that, I tell them, there's no connection between fitness and moral superiority, which is not of course the Roman view.

I follow at a more stately pace, burdened with the day's food and water and coats in case the weather changes, taking time to imagine the Syrian regiment that built this section. It's hard enough carrying a day-bag for four up and down there. You certainly wouldn't move stones unless the army said you had to, and so there they have stayed since the North African conscripts left them. I suppose the foot soldiers of any empire have trenchant views about their orders, but this one must have seemed particularly bonkers. The southern side of Whin Sill is a grassy slope steep enough for us to picnic later at the top in reasonable confidence that curious cows won't make it up. That was the Roman side, and became the English side. The northern aspect is a vertical drop of over 300 feet, the edge of the old lava flow. We pause for my older son, a rock-climber, to map out how he'd do it if he had the kit, but it's not remotely plausible as a route of attack or even sheep rustling. It was wholly unnecessary to add a ten-feet-high wall at the top, even more to go on placing the milecastles at exact intervals regardless of any practical consideration. There's a strange conversation going on here between the political will of Rome and the mineral reality of dolerite, a manufacture of meaning that doesn't quite work.

The people who built and then policed the wall came from all over this empire, only a small minority from Rome itself. The regiment that built a section of this English landmark came from Syria in the first century AD. Roman-era memorial stones in Northumberland, Yorkshire and Cumbria commemorate the lives of people from North Africa and what we now call the Middle East. I know I said I was going to try not to do things like this, but I am irresistibly tempted to suggest that the classical bedrock of English history is as much a thing of flux and mutability as the bedrock of our border. They weren't really 'the Romans', just people from everywhere under Roman command, followed later by people who came over other seas following other orders. Whin Sill, like any igneous rock, is just where things happened to cool and set and therefore where we fought some wars. It wasn't ordained that way.

Especially, I guess, on the edges of a continent, especially in times of trouble when nations want simple stories about themselves, we want the stones under our feet to fall into line, to tell us what we want to hear about time and space. That is what the Romans wanted from Whin Sill, a geological underwriting for this tenuous and briefly held outpost of empire. And I want the opposite, a sermon in stone that says we all come from everywhere and that nationhood is just a story that is sometimes convenient. But basalt and dolerite, the firestones, don't really mean anything. They are just there, for lengths of time that make the rise and fall of the Roman Empire happen in a breath, the British Empire too short to register at all. I don't find much comfort in that thought – since we invented nuclear war we have lost the capacity to reassure ourselves that everything has happened before and the world goes on, and climate change is only a more gradual version of man-made apocalypse. Whin Sill won't last forever, but the continents will go on pushing and pulling, the firestone far beneath our feet bubbling and seeping, the raw material of creation on the move.

Rock Talk

CANADIAN ARCTIC

Sara Wheeler

O ur Twin Otter approached a tiny camp and a rope of caribou spooled away from the din of the engine: from the air, you could not see the gallop. The animals flowed in an eternal stream. The less eternal plane bounced hard before ramming itself to a stop. Three geologists and I climbed down a ladder into sheet rain that fell horizontally. Instead of the clean snow, sharp air and zero precipitation of the proper Arctic, we contemplated mud, fog and drizzle. Washed of all colour except dun, the landscape could not have looked bleaker.

A figure swaddled in dripping Gore-Tex appeared dragging a banana sledge. Four sodden kitbags sat on it, with our tents in them. There was nothing to be done but put them up. So we battled with waterlogged – and anachronistic – canvas, arcing poles and semi-freddo soil in driving rain and wind, all four of us casting longing glances at the Otter as it taxied away, leaving us in that wind-blasted, soaking, cold place at the end, as it seemed to us, of the known world.

Southampton Island in the Canadian Arctic covers 15,700 square miles, or 41,439 square kilometres, and, with a cluster of smaller islands, corks what is in effect Canada's fourth ocean – Hudson Bay and its drain-like appendage, James Bay. As an itinerant writer with a commission to write a book about the circumpolar Arctic, I had been invited to join a publicly funded geoscientific mapping project on Southampton Island. Twenty geologists were camping there for ten weeks, supported by two helicopters.

Much later on that miserable first day, the rain stopped. The sun came out, spangling the Kirchoffer River, and I sat on an empty fuel drum watching geologists disgorge from the choppers after a hard day in the field. Camp consisted of twenty Logan tents that had once been white, two lavatory tents positioned at a safe distance, a shower tent deploying a Heath Robinson-style system of pulleys and buckets to empty an old fuel drum of tepid water over one's head, a gabled cook tent and an identical 'office tent'.

Each night before supper, the geologists gathered in the office tent for a group assessment of the day's work. In the middle section of the tent, a bristling bank of charging satellite phones and radios took up one whole wall, each device plugged into a rack of power bars that sucked energy for the eight hours each day that the lone generator was operational. This vital evening session was called Rock Talk. The scientists went out on foot every day, if the weather let them, and at Rock Talk they each described what they had observed, passing round sample lumps for inspection (someone described one rock as 'maple-sugary bronze'), speculating on the rocks' origins and evaluating the implications of what they had found.

The day after I arrived I went on a bedrock traverse with Joyia, the project co-leader, and Joe, an old hand from the Geological Survey of Canada, a branch of Natural Resources Canada, not an insignificant government department in a country with more natural resources than it knows what to do with. Joyia was a sanguine figure who looked younger than her thirty-two years. She exuded serenity, had welcomed me warmly to camp – indeed it was she who had invited me, valuing a small collaboration between the legendarily separated two cultures of art and science. Over the next two weeks we were often to stand on the tundra and have a talk last thing at night over a final cigarette.

At about ten o'clock, a chopper dropped us a couple of miles to the south-west of camp and we started hiking across a plain surrounded by low hills and glacial outwash deposits. The sky was flawless, and mist rose from a livid blue lake. We had walked some way from our first data-logging station and just arrived at our second. It was well above zero degrees with no windchill, and our backs were sweaty under the packs. As we began getting out the observational instrumentation, Joyia stiffened. She said, 'Bear'. I tasted again the coffee I had drunk at breakfast. Around half a mile away, a polar bear was loping up an escarpment.

We had been downwind of him for an hour, so he must have smelt us, and after a few minutes he lifted his snout in the air, and began to circle. Half a mile might seem like a long way, but when there is nothing between you and a bear that can outrun you, it is a very short distance indeed. Joyia cocked the gun, and Joe and I loaded anti-bear firecrackers that allegedly frighten the beasts into running away (an improbable outcome, I always thought). Half the world's polar bears hunt in the province of Nunavut. But only one mattered. We called camp on a satphone, asking for a pilot to come and get us. The bear completed a quarter circle, and disappeared over a ridge. We kept vigil, and chatted. Joe looked at rocks; it was difficult to say whether his nonchalance was studied. Joyia alternately scanned the horizon with field glasses and fiddled with her Brunton compass. Then we heard the *thwock-thwock* of the helicopter. It was a good sound. Before we could see the machine, Joyia made radio contact. The pilot had found the bear, and nudged him to the other side of a lake. The chopper landed, and dropped off Noah, one of our local bear monitors (more of them later), as he was going to spend the rest of the day with us, increasing our gun quotient. We continued.

That night, when the students were washing up, I talked to Don James, head of the Canada-Nunavut Geoscience Office and the most senior scientist in camp, an articulate and friendly individual whom everybody liked. I asked him why so much public money was being pumped into mapping an almost empty slab of rock and tundra. 'We're assisting mineral exploration companies,' he said, perching on an oil drum next to me, 'by gathering data so they know where to start looking. The end product of a season of traverses and months of processing work in the labs will be a map of the bedrock of the island on a scale of 1:250,000. Our main aim is to see what the land can produce in the way of natural resources which will stimulate an economy.' An acrid smell arose from the socks drying over the stove rail. I asked if the team were looking for oil and gas.

'Basically, yes,' James continued. 'The geologists concerned might not have oil and gas in mind, but those using the data later will interpret it for that. We're hopeful that there might be diamonds and base metals here too.'

The Inuit had harvested their environment for many centuries, curing seal hides with spittle; catching bowhead with bone harpoons; conjuring gods and spirits from the ice to invest the universe with meaning. Southern interlopers came for whale oil, then blue fox fur, then hydrocarbons, and now diamonds and gold. As the rock showed, time passed in the blink of an eye. Oil will one day join the list of exhausted resources.

On the way to one traverse, over the chopper headset I heard the others talking about 'the coast', and pointing. I was travelling with Doug, a senior scientist from the Geological Survey. Doug had spent hundreds of months tramping over Arctic tundra looking at rocks. With all this talk of coast I peered out, squinting at a jellied sun in a failed attempt to spot any sea, any beach, anywhere where land might conceivably end.

Over squished lunchtime ham sandwiches, I asked Doug about his earlier remarks. 'We were talking about the coast 7,000 years ago,' he said, as if that were a normal activity, which for them, it was. But in the end we did arrive somewhere recognisably coastal. It was the top of the cliffs of Duke of York Bay, looking out at a crescent-shaped beach. Doug strode around the outcrops brandishing his instruments, eventually homing in on a patch of whaleback rock formations. 'These,' he told me, kneeling to scrape off lichen, 'are illustrative of former glacier-covered land. And these' – he pointed at a set of parallel lines etched into the rock – 'are striations.' Formed when debris at the base of flowing glacier ice scours the bedrock, striations reveal the direction in which a glacier moved. 'If we can provide that directional information for mining companies,' Doug continued, 'they will have more of an idea of where to look.' So the rocks spoke a language of their own. Unlike the other languages of Nunavut, this one brought development and wealth and other things that wreck a landscape. At least for a few brief lifetimes.

It was 7°C when we gathered for breakfast the next day, and the bugs were dense in the fresh morning air. Ah yes, the bugs. The pages of my notebook tell their own story, encrusted with flattened mosquito and blackfly corpses and splodges of my own blood. The bugs bit us even when we wore jackets with full-head net hoods and peered out at the landscape through a veil of brown mesh. But soon sharp, heavy rain squalls unfurled across the tundra, painting the landscape grey. The horizon dissolved, and the world turned to a miasma of opaque vapour. When the raincloud rolled back, the distant rocks shone, as if they had been varnished. If that happened in the early morning, as it often did, our hopes of getting out on a traverse rose, like milk to the boil. But the rain always came back. On my tenth day, it pinned us in camp. The pilots went off to read what they referred to as heli-porn (this turned out to be a stack of magazines called *Vertical*). The scientists retaliated with geo-porn:

magazines about hammers, drills, screws and shafts. The pendulum swung between freezing wind and warmish calm inhabited by dark billions of mosquitoes. For a few heavenly moments every day, the pendulum looped through the midway point, and there were no bugs, no lacerating wind. But you couldn't really enjoy the interlude, because you knew what was coming next.

The earliest-known residents of Southampton, the Sadleirmiut, called their island Shugliak, which means 'puppy suckling' (or 'island-puppy suckling mother-continent'). The Sadleirmiut died out at the beginning of the twentieth century when they contracted an unknown disease from whalers. Then, hundreds of generations connecting people to the land expired in a heartbeat. In the 1920s, the Hudson's Bay Company built a fur post on the island and shipped in Aivilimmiut and Uqqurmiut from Baffin Island and elsewhere to service trade. The descendants of these two groups still live in Coral Harbour, the only settlement on Southampton Island, situated on an inlet on the south coast. I referred earlier to 'bear monitors' recruited from Coral Harbour. These positions were rotated between any man who fancied the job. It was a token gesture, as the monitors never really did anything, but they were a friendly presence in camp. Inuit owned the land, not the geologists, and in effect, the monitors' wages represented blood money. And why not?

Monitors Chris and Noah both came with us on one traverse. On the chopper they talked about playing Poker Stars on the internet. We put down next to a pair of rounded, symmetrical hills that earlier hunters had named The Buttocks. Canadian Arctic toponyms often record the place where things happened. They do in most languages, but Inuit have no misgivings – thus Pisspot, or Where Robert Broke Wind Loudly. As we climbed out of the machine, a bull caribou raced up and down behind us, his harem of splay-footed cows and their calves observing from a safe distance. The Buttocks region was noted for its hunting, and Noah and Chris speculated on the high-summer availability of caribou. Noah was thirty-two and the taller, less confident Chris, twenty-eight. Neither had ever been outside Nunavut. They both loved talking about hunting. With their families they kept, cooperatively, nine working dog teams in Coral Harbour, but most people went out on snowmobiles instead of mushing; either that or on quad bikes. Noah and Chris shot bearded seal, walrus, narwhal, caribou, hare, tundra swan, snow geese, sandhill cranes, eider duck and king eider. 'My freezer is full of caribou jerky,' said Noah. His eight-year-old son had recently shot his first narwhal.

Buried amid restrictive quotas, alternative food supplies, the economic demands of a family and the blandishments of the internet, the dream of the Arctic hunter still flickered.

That evening one or two people swam in the river. I went fishing with Noah, and got two landlocked char which he threw back in, claiming that only the ocean-going variety were worth eating. One of the fish snagged on a saputit, a stone weir built in shallow water by some ancestral Inuit to catch the sardine-like *angmagiaq*, which make an annual spawning run up the inlets. When we walked back, half the camp was in shadow. In the other half, evening sunlight intensified the tundra colours on the ground, deepening the tents to French grey.

At that night's Rock Talk one group told stories of a browned circle they had found that was once an Inuit tent ring. Don James reckoned it was 5,000 years old. A flinty limestone tool still lay there that someone had once used for scraping. Nobody seemed surprised. The past was not a foreign country to them; it was somewhere they visited often. As the Canadian novelist Robertson Davies put it in his 1972 novel *The Manticore*, 'None of us counts for much in the long, voiceless, inert history of the stone'.

Granite

DARTMOOR

Peter Randall-Page

I have lived and worked on Dartmoor for more than a quarter of a century and the underlying geology of the place has affected my day-to-day experience of the landscape as well as my practice as an artist.

Since childhood I have been fascinated by the variety and beauty of natural phenomena and over the years have become increasingly interested in the fundamental themes that underpin the seemingly infinite variations of forms that nature produces: the exquisite forms of shells echoing the spiralling turbulence of water in the Dartmoor streams; the hexagonal packing of honeycombs and the basalt columns of the Giant's Causeway. The same geometric forms appear again and again in disparate contexts resulting from entirely unrelated physical processes.

It is almost as if phenomena, both organic and inorganic, are drawn from a kind of pattern book of basic forms, which are best understood in terms of geometry. Yet nature resists exact repetition: no two oak leaves, pebbles or human faces are identical. Spontaneous pattern formation is always mitigated by random variation. In fact the evolutionary process itself is driven by this tension between underlying themes and variations produced by random mutation.

The same ordering principles pervade both organic and inorganic form in obedience to the laws of physics. Human beings are pattern-recognising creatures, and in our attempt to make sense of the world we like to categorise things, in terms of their kinship, the genus and species of living things for example. As we know, however, this rigid compartmentalising only works at a particular moment in time, as everything is constantly metamorphosing into something else, be it the evolution of one organism into another or the constant changing of the Earth in a geological timescale.

In this sense the drawing of rigid lines of distinction between phenomena is not the whole story. We consider some things to be alive or organic and others to be inert and inorganic, but at some time in the past that distinction must have been buried when dumb matter took on a spark of life and the ability to replicate.

Granite is stuff personified. Quintessentially dumb matter, it is what the Earth is made of: congealed magma, planetary and galactic, inert and unintelligible. Of course, the tors and boulders of Dartmoor bear witness to their own stories: the molten magma intruding into the country sediments and cooling slowly deep in the crust, cooling so slowly that feldspar crystals had time to grow enormous. Cooling and shrinking produced rectilinear three-dimensional cracks. Erosion eventually wore away the softer rock leaving a kind of cast.

The tors of Dartmoor can seem more like the ruins of some ancient civilisation with a passion for monumental masonry. In fact the appearance of something constructed from large blocks was produced by totally different processes: flowing, cooling, shrinking and eroding.

Igneous rock in general and granite in particular can be seen as the mother of all rocks. Eroding and decaying granite produces gravel, sand and china clay, which together with shells and other organic debris produce sediments, and eventually under pressure form sedimentary rocks such as sandstone and limestone. In turn, some of these sedimentary rocks crystallise under heat and pressure deep in the earth to produce metamorphic rocks like marble.

My own interest in geology goes back to childhood when I was a keen fossil collector. As an eight-year-old amateur palaeontologist I wrote to the Natural History Museum in London to express my passion for fossils and ask advice about where to go hunting for them. To my and my parents amazement I received a box by post from the Head of Palaeontology, containing about a dozen beautiful fossils, which became the basis for my fossil collection, and which I still have to this day.

My interest in stone as a material for sculpture was kindled a few years later at another great London institution, the British Museum. I became particularly interested in prehistoric figurines, which seem to me to embody something fundamental about the human condition. I also became obsessed by Egyptian sculpture and spent many hours drawing in the Egyptian monumental galleries.

The Ancient Egyptians chose to use the most incredibly hard granites and basalts for their sculpture. Without the benefit of steel tools they used other hard stones and later bronze tools, which were incapable of cutting into the material. Instead they achieved their exquisite carving through a kind of controlled erosion, wearing away the rock by chipping and grinding.

The result is understated forms, which have a great sense of inner energy, drawing the imagination from the surface into the dark, dense interior of the stone. My passion for stone carving was confirmed when I was taken on a school trip to Paris where I discovered the reconstructed studio of the Romanian sculptor Constantin Brancusi in the basement of the Musée d'Art Moderne. Brancusi's work was a revelation; his honed and refined forms with their internalised energy had the same effect on me as the Egyptian sculptures, and I knew at once that I wanted to be part of this kind of endeavour.

My father was a model maker and, as a severely dyslexic child, I spent much of my time helping him in his garden-shed studio or making things of my own. I have been a maker for as long as I can remember, and sculpture was always what I wanted to do.

I studied sculpture at Bath Academy of Art in the mid 1970s and experimented with many different materials and techniques during my four years as a student there. It was only towards the end of my time at college that I discovered Bath stone and my interest in carving was reawakened.

I am drawn to the conceptual simplicity of the carving process, removing everything extraneous to the desired form. It is a one-way process and, as in life, there is no going back; one must redeem any errors by moving on into the stone.

Carving is also a meditative process, which is conducive to a fluid dialogue between appraisal, action and reappraisal. The body is busy with a repetitive task and, rather like walking, this can liberate the imagination in an unselfconscious pursuit of form.

After leaving art school, I worked for a few years on the conservation and restoration of the thirteenth-century west front of Wells Cathedral and became immersed in the beautiful, semi-abstract forms of foliage and drapery that characterise so much medieval sculpture.

In the early 1980s, I won a Churchill fellowship to study marble carving near Carrara, in Italy, where I learned the technique of triangulation using compasses as a way of scaling up from a maquette.

My love affair with granite only really began when my wife and I moved to Dartmoor with our two young children in 1987. In retrospect I have worked my way back in geological time in my choice of stone, beginning with the relatively young sedimentary limestone of Bath, through the metamorphic marble of Carrara to the most ancient material of granite.

All materials have inherent potentialities and limitations, by their very nature. Granite does not lend itself to Hellenistic or Baroque flights of fantasy or romantic gesture. Granite is conducive to a heavy understated sensuality, fecundity rather than frippery. Because of the hardness and brittleness of its crystalline structure, it can be split using special wedges called plugs and feathers, and it can be worked using a pitching tool which results in a natural cleft or riven surface.

My first use of Dartmoor granite on moving to Devon was for a project commissioned by the innovative environmental arts charity 'Common Ground'. They called the project 'Local Distinctiveness' and the idea was to place small works of the imagination in and around the Teign Valley on publicly accessible land in the immediate vicinity of my home. I wanted people to come across these sculptures with a sense of personal encounter and discovery, without signage or interpretation boards, rather like a secular version of the shrines and *genius loci* sculptures of southern Europe and Asia.

I liked the idea of using indigenous materials without physically adding anything alien, but rather revealing a space within the existing elements of the landscape in which to make my interventions. I thought of using the naturally eroded boulders which are strewn everywhere across the Dartmoor landscape. By splitting one of these boulders in half I was able to reveal a new space within an existing element of the place. The first piece I made, entitled *Granite Song*, was made from a fairly small boulder (about 80 centimetres in diameter), in which I carved the split faces of the stone with a sensuous mirror-image pattern carved in low relief on both surfaces. The sculpture is sited on a small island in the River Teign. The stone is exactly like the boulders that form the riverbed itself, but split to 'reveal' unexpected internal structures implied by my carving on the split faces.

Being so hard and intractable, granite can withstand erosion by glaciation or other forms of weathering. This produces naturally rounded forms, which maintain their physical integrity like giant beach pebbles.

I went on to make a series of split-boulder works and subsequently used the natural shape of boulders as a random starting point, carving low-relief, often geometric, patterns over their entire surface. I became interested in the way natural phenomena seem to spring from a tension between an ordering principle and random variation. In this sense, the boulder represents the random element created by countless chance events on a geological timescale, where the surface pattern is the ordering principle which must yield and adapt to the vagaries of the shape of the rock.

For me, one of the most important qualities of granite is that it is quintessentially stuff, with no element of organic life. I like the challenge of imbuing what we consider to be something absolutely lifeless with a sense of vitality and human meaning.

In 2003, I began work on my largest and most ambitious granite sculpture commissioned by the Eden Project in Cornwall. I was invited to work with Jolyon Brewis from Grimshaw Architects on the designing of a new education building incorporating a sculpture. The Eden Project is dedicated to exploring our vital symbiotic relationship with the natural world in general and plants in particular. Our challenge was to incorporate botanical imagery and symbolism into both building and sculpture.

For many years I have been interested in the underlying geometric principles that govern plant growth. One of the most fascinating and complex patterns found in plants is known as 'spiral phyllotaxis', which determines the shape of pinecones and arrangements of leaves on a stem. Its most obvious manifestation is in the packing of seeds in a sunflower head, and results from the imperative for efficient pattern developed over millennia of evolutionary natural selection.

We started to experiment with spiral phyllotaxis as the basis for a roof structure with a chamber at its centre, housing an enormous granite sculpture based on the same plant geometry as the roof. The clients, quite rightly, wanted to use local Cornish granite for the sculpture and it took over a year to find a quarry willing to excavate a large enough stone. De Lank Quarry on Bodmin Moor agreed to quarry a stone weighing 167 tonnes. My team and I then worked for two years at the quarry. We designed a lathe to remove the majority of the waste material and carved thousands of raised nodules in accordance with the complex growth pattern.

Eventually, after we had removed over a hundred tonnes of material from the original block, the finished sculpture was craned into the purpose-built chamber at the heart of the new building.

My next project in granite was installed in a London square built on the site of the old Middlesex Hospital, just north of Oxford Street. It involved a large natural boulder from Germany, measuring 3.5 metres tall and weighing 25 tonnes. I've been using granite from a quarry in the Bavarian forest on and off for some years because of the thousands of beautifully, rounded stones that are strewn in huge piles throughout the site. The whole excavation is overburdened with boulders ranging from half a metre to 3, 4 or even 5 metres in diameter. Their rounded shape is not the result of glaciation, but of 'onion skin' weathering.

I am no geologist, but it looks as if, at some time in geological history, these rocks were exposed to extreme temperature fluctuations, heating the outer layer of the rock, causing it to expand and eventually break away in layers, like peeling an onion.

They call these stones 'findlings', orphan boulders, separated from mother bedrock and having to fend for themselves in the elements, their corners knocked off by heat, cold, wind and rain, until their outlines become softened and their surface-to-volume ratio reduced by the abrasion of time.

The need to find meaning in the world seems fundamental to the human condition and one could argue that art, science and religion all spring from the same basic desire to make sense of things.

We are pattern-recognising creatures and imbue the world with form and meaning through our art, music and literature. We are also mark-making creatures, and communicate our beliefs, hopes, fears and ideas through drawing and writing; incising, daubing, inscribing, printing and scratching onto papyrus, bark, paper, clay and of course stone.

Granite is our planetary bedrock, our mother Earth, the substance on whose surface we live out our short lives. In many ways, granite is indifferent, unintelligible and impenetrable to us. The geological timescale that governs its metamorphosis from molten magma via tors and boulders to pebbles, gravel and sand operates on an unimaginably long timescale compared to our own flash of vitality between womb and tomb.

The marks we make on stone imbue it with meaning and render it intelligible. In the past, I have used the random shape of the boulder as a starting point – incising onto the surface geometric patterns which have to morph and distort to accommodate the shape of the stone. But on the piece installed in London, I used writing systems as pattern and text as texture.

Whereas spoken language is thought to have developed from one single system, written language seems to have at least three distinct and unrelated origins – in Mesopotamia, China and Central America. They must have emerged to deal with the social and economic complexity of running the first cities, and the earliest forms of writing tend to be do with accountancy and IOUs. Very soon, however, the newfound ability to communicate over time and space by mark-making spawned more imaginative uses.

All cultures have creation myths and some of the earliest written texts are an attempt to imagine the unimaginable: where did we come from, and how did it all begin? And my sculpture bears the opening lines of creation stories from each culture – from the very earliest cuneiform of ancient Mesopotamia to the present day.

By making marks on stones we make them part of our world – an affirmation of our own brief existence. At the very least, it is an assertion that I was here.

From Taiga to Tundra
SIBERIA
Daniel Kalder

G rowing up in the UK, I never felt that nature was terrifying, or even slightly frightening. There were some cold bits up north, but they were not that cold – certainly not compared to the North Pole. The mountains were not that tall, the forest was not that vast and nothing in it was going to kill you. There were no wolves, no bears, no highly poisonous snakes, just creatures from *The Wind in the Willows*. You know: badgers, toads, the odd hedgehog – nothing lethal. Even our legends are benign: what lurks in the forest? Why it's only Robin Hood and his Merry Men, and they rob from the rich to give to the poor: nice guys. In Britain, the landscape is our friend. We have fenced it in with hedgerows, filled it with sheep. We have tamed it. How disappointing.

Now in Russia, it's different. I moved there in the mid 1990s in deep winter, and immediately realised that this was a landscape too vast and wild ever to be rendered quaint. The essence of its ferocity was summed up for me during a visit to the city of Arkhangelsk in the far north – again, in the depths of winter. It was cold, incredibly cold – and also very, very dark. And when it wasn't dark, a thick mist rolled in from the White Sea to conceal things I needed to see. Beyond Arkhangelsk, there was thick forest and beyond that, a world of ice where only polar bears dared to tread.

One day I met the city's chief architect, an affable professor of Soviet vintage, who said something that resonated with me deeply: 'Russian culture is defined by a fear of the forest.' There was something very alien about those words; they were completely un-British, that's for sure. But I immediately grasped what he was talking about. There is nothing cosy about Russian nature. There is too much of it; it cannot be reined in. Its dangerous magic is contained in their stories: one of the most famous characters in Russian folklore is Baba Yaga, a witch who lives in the forest in a house on chicken legs. She roasts children in her stove. Then there is the Leshii, a spirit who lures unsuspecting victims into the forest, leading them in circles until they are lost. And there are plenty of other, deeply evil spirits lurking in the unseen places.

This fear of the forest, this terror of nature resonated with me for another reason. The month before, I'd been in Siberia. Now European Russia is big, but Siberia exists on another plane of big entirely. It seems to stretch on forever: across vast lakes and rivers, over weird land-oceans of steppe and up into immense stretches of Arctic ice. And, of course, there is the forest, or taiga. People have been vanishing into it for years, fleeing the Antichrist, or oppression, or the oppression of the Antichrist. Centuries pass, and then explorers discover the great-great grandchildren of these exiles, asking in old dialects why there is no Tsar.

I was in Siberia to visit a religious community whose members believed that a former Soviet traffic cop was the Son of God. The Messiah lived on top of a mountain, close to the sky, but his thousands of followers lived on the Earth in small villages surrounded by the taiga. Now, until this point, I had never quite seen the purpose of that word 'taiga': why not just translate it as 'forest'? But here I could see its necessity. It wasn't about 'biomes' or types of tree. It was the sense of immensity and severity, and danger. The trees were incredibly tall and dark and dense, and standing in their serried ranks, they glowered at me.

Yes, the villagers had cut out a little clearing, but their tiny settlement was ready to be engulfed at any moment. This human creation was all so fragile, just as all the villages erected in defiance of terrible nature across the centuries had been fragile. Fearing the forest made sense; it would be stupid not to fear it, especially because this ominous, threatening and entirely natural great wall of Siberia was also mesmerising. In fact, the taiga called to me, and its call was strong. The trees concealed secrets, and I wanted to uncover them. But this was the siren song that invited you to jump off a cliff, or stick your hand in the fire. And as it is, the taiga spoke with more than one voice. Those trees also warned me: *Do not come in here. There is no way out. O British person, there are no friendly badgers here.*

However, there are poisonous berries, and clouds of mosquitoes, and wolves, and bears – don't forget the bears. I mean, I'm a town boy; nobody ever taught me how to navigate by the stars, or how to trap and skin an animal, or which mushrooms are safe to eat. Hardly anybody knows that stuff in the UK any more; we industrialised so long ago. And the sense of danger was not my outsider's hallucination: the villagers stuck studiously to their paths, avoiding direct encounters with the taiga. I was told the cautionary tale of a young girl who wandered into the trees and, swallowed by the dark immensity – or perhaps a bear – was never seen again. Even the traffic-cop Messiah, plugged directly into the godhead and blessed with a supra-human understanding of all things, was powerless to help.

But the truth is, the taiga is hardly the most brutal of the landscapes that the peoples of Russia have to contend with. There is also the steppe – those vast, flat grassy plains that stretch on forever. Good luck surviving there without advanced nomad skills and an extended clan structure to support you. And to the north lies a landscape far, far more brutal: the tundra, where animals and plants eke out a difficult existence in an uncompromisingly hostile environment. An ice desert. You'll love it if you're lichen.

When I think of the tundra, I first think of the cold. I know the cold pretty well, but in the tundra, 'extreme' takes on an entirely different meaning. And since most Westerners are only ever visitors to that bleak land, we struggle to get a true sense of it. How cold is that cold really? Varlaam Shalamov was a Soviet writer who spent seventeen years in the labour camps in north-eastern Siberia. He knew the cold intimately. This is how he puts it in his *Kolyma Tales*:

> If there was frosty fog, that meant the temperature outside was forty degrees below zero; if you exhaled easily but in a rasping fashion, it was fifty degrees below zero; if there was a rasping and it was difficult to breathe, it was sixty degrees below; after sixty degrees below zero, spit froze in mid-air.

That's cold. And the ground, too, is cold. Beneath a shallow surface layer it never thaws and, like the taiga, demands a word of its own: permafrost. But even the bit that does thaw is deprived of nutrients, as dead plants and animals don't decompose very well in the tundra. They horde all their corpsey goodness to themselves, prevented by the freezing temperatures from sharing the precious treasures of organic dissolution with the earth. The cold even blocks rocks from doing much eroding and thus the soil is starved further. That is not to say the situation is entirely hopeless; the tundra is not sterile. For instance, shrubs and grass and berries survive, and there are deer and birds. But living things must stay close to the soil; any frosty Icarus that attempts to rise up will be killed by exposure.

Now this is a landscape to fear, yet still I am drawn to the tundra. Perhaps what I like most about it is that the permafrost functions like a giant geological sofa. Not in that it is comfortable; it certainly is not – but in that things can slip down thc back of it and bc forgotten for a long time, only to turn up a few millennia later when you are least expecting it.

For instance, in Saint Petersburg's zoological museum there is a glass case containing the remains of the Berezovka mammoth, which was discovered in north-eastern Siberia in 1900. By 'remains' I mean bits of its skin have been stretched over a model of questionable quality. For years I would make pilgrimages to this relic. I loved its story: a hunter spotted its head sticking out of the dirt; it was sufficiently fresh that bits of food were still stuck between its molars, and wolves could eat the exposed parts. Eventually the creature was excavated and dispatched on a train to the capital where the carcass enjoyed an audience with the Imperial Couple. The Empress disliked the smell. A decade and a half later the Bolsheviks shot her. They kept the mammoth.

Since then many woolly mammoths have turned up in the tundra, so many that we are awash with mammoth ivory and its trade is completely legal. We are also awash with mammoth DNA, and may eventually clone one because – well – what could possibly go wrong? Perhaps one day, too, scientists will clone a woolly rhinoceros, and – why not? – every other type of creature that lies preserved in the frozen ground. Why, we could even clone the grim-faced Soviet bureaucrats who ran the gulags, but who now lie sleeping in the ice, bedecked in medals, all those thousands and thousands of dialectical materialist mummies. And once they are reborn, will we still be able to see the blood on their hands?

But there is more preserved beneath the tundra than dead mammals. More dangerous are the ancient viruses. Last year, a thirty-thousand-year-old strain was thawed out and swiftly became infectious again. Fortunately it could only attack amoebas, but there are surely other, more lethal, threats down there: ancient strains of smallpox, for instance, which we humans in our arrogance believe we eradicated in the 1970s. In fact, the permafrost has been retreating since the 1970s, so we will see more of these diseases, zombie microbes rising again to lay waste to the human species, or even, perhaps, to kill the reborn mammoths all over again.

In fact, so strange and dangerous and perplexing is the tundra, that it is increasingly full of holes, which simply erupt, inexplicably, out of the earth. No, really: Russian scientists have identified seven of these craters, the largest of which is a mile and a half across – although the area is so sparsely populated that there could be many more. Some fear that the craters are created by subterranean methane explosions, caused by the warming climate, which in turn will release still more methane into the atmosphere, warming the Earth further, melting more of the permafrost, releasing more of its dangers.

So there are dead things and diseases and giant holes leaking gas. But there is also treasure in the Siberian tundra. The ground is rich in oil, coal, diamonds, gold and precious rocks and metals, all those great seams of wealth which can be used to make beautiful things but also inspire humans to behave badly. This is what attracted European Russians to settle in areas that had previously been occupied by reindeer-herding Evenk, or the shamanistic Yakut people, among others. The glittering caves, the buried treasure. The far eastern republic of Sakha is home to ninety-nine percent of Russia's diamonds, and it is there that you can find my favourite hole in the world, the Mirny open-cast diamond mine, which is almost a mile across and nearly 2,000 feet deep. When the Soviets were digging it out in the 1950s, the permafrost was so resistant they tried melting it with jet engines, and when that failed they blasted it with explosives, raging at the earth to get at its buried treasure. Mirny was abandoned in the mid 2000s, although a city remains perched on the edge of it, and mining continues underground.

In the nineteenth century, the tsars used penal labour to dig out the tundra's gold, while under Stalin, slave colonies were established to fuel the USSR's rise to become the second-largest gold producer in the world. Magadan was the administrative centre of the northernmost camps in the Kolyma region, a grim collection of Soviet blocks. Cruelty and darkness and great ugliness permeated Magadan, and yet Vadim Kozin, a Soviet singer who was exiled there in the 1950s, wrote a song comparing its boulevards to those of Paris. I remain unpersuaded.

However, although the tundra is truly terrifying, I confess I think it wrong to speak of the landscape exclusively in terms of fear. I mentioned earlier that there are groups of peoples who have inhabited these cold regions for a very long time, among them the Chukchi, a polar people who were the butt of racist jokes in Soviet times, much as the Irish used to be in Britain. For me, it was a Chukchi author who hinted at a different way of relating to the ice desert. In Yuri Rytkheu's *Chukchi Bible* he tells the story of his shaman ancestors and the world they inhabited – which they believed had been formed from the droppings of a divine raven. As a post-industrial European, it was a reality as alien to me as that of any science fiction novel – more so even, as science fiction is always extrapolated from the world I know.

Rytkheu's book was full of wind and ice and birds; of walrus meat and cloaks made of walrus intestines; of hunting and violence and long nights spent telling stories in the interminable and impenetrable darkness. It was a world of ritual and eternal return, of gods and visions and a sense of place as deep as the permafrost. Above all, that world was imbued for its inhabitants with a sense of the sacred. Thus, if there was terror, it was in the sublime sense, of fear commingled with awe and reverence. That is something which, in my view, you cannot feel when you have divided and subdivided and fenced in a landscape, filling it with sheep and pretty parks run by the National Trust. I'm not saying I would ever choose to live in the tundra; I wouldn't. But I respect the wise fear of those who do.

Quartz

UDAL PENINSULA & BEN LAWERS

Linda Cracknell

In the summer of 2016 I part-rode, part-pushed my bicycle, loaded with a tent and some art materials, across the narrow waist of the Udal peninsula on the Hebridean island of North Uist. I was heading for the dunes that frame the crescent of west-facing Traigh Iar, one of those glorious shell-sand beaches that sing white in sunshine.

I abandoned my bicycle to walk barefoot. With two miles of beach to myself, I went north towards a widening series of headlands and dunes where a number of archaeological excavation sites, opened over a thirty-year period from the early 1960s, remain exposed. It was low tide, the August day warm and overcast, offering expansive horizontal stripes of graded greys and blues, the misty peaks of Harris ahead. There was a melancholy to the emptiness.

A line of tangled weed marked the high-tide line, and a foot or so below this, the sea had cast up a parallel band of glossy pebbles. I began to collect, quickly getting my eye in, spotting the gleam of damp, worn quartz among other stones. I gathered them according to how pleasing they felt in my hand, the cool on my palm and their translucent, milky colour. Once they were collected into a cloth bag, I enjoyed their music, clacking against each other as I walked. The word 'quartz' comes to us from Slavic languages through German, meaning 'hard'. This trait makes it the dominant mineral of mountaintops and the main constituent of beach, river and desert sand.

Excavations at Udal revealed a palimpsest of dwellings; continuous occupation from Neolithic times through to the nineteenth century. Among the finds were two quartz pebbles painted with curved lines and dots. Fifty-six of these enigmatic objects have been found around Scotland; all but five in Caithness, Orkney and Shetland. They range in date from the first century to the ninth century AD. Experimental archaeology suggests the pigment may be associated with metal workers, and made from distilled peat tar which penetrated the surface of the stone, leaving a ghost-stain.

The emblematic value of quartz in prehistory is well known, but it is not known whether these scarce decorated stones were charms of some sort – perhaps for healing, or slingshots, or perhaps even part of a game. They were certainly portable. Might they have been used as gifts, or for trading, even a type of currency? I like the fact that no one knows, that imagination is required.

The incoming tide gave me a sense of urgency. My walk had magicked up a rough plan, a game I would play with the tides. I chose my favourite twenty-five pebbles, the whitest ones, the most smoothed. I let them dry for a short time and then painted each with waterproof ink. I used a wide palette, imitating patterns I had seen on the ancient pebbles – the saltire-like arrangements of curved lines and dots, other simple motifs. I also had twenty-five words in mind and inscribed these, one on the reverse of each pebble. Each word had some relevance to the place I was in and the story of migrating sand and memory. One excavated site has already been lost to an Atlantic storm; despite the many years of passionate endeavour here, the discoveries made were not published at the time and the memory of what was learned looked threatened.

Finally, as the sea retreated, I settled my grid of stones below the high-tide line. I laid them, pattern up, in a five-by-five square, echoing the grids used to record on archaeological sites. Each pebble was distinct but I loved them together, luminous on the sand with the evening sun milkily suggesting itself out west. It looked like an eccentric board game, a hoard of sweeties, or as if it awaited a casting of the runes. I would return after the next high tide, a chunk of time for which I needed no watch. I was excited to see which words the sea would select for me; my 'found poem'.

I woke at one in the morning, looked out of my tent at a bright full moon, heard waves soothing at some distance. It was approximately low tide. And I slept again, warm with the knowledge of my pebbles glinting under moonlight on the sand below, left to their tidal dance.

By half nine the next morning the sea had been in and out, far enough to reveal its choices. I ran down onto the still-wet sands, wandered the pebble line, and identified quartz pebbles whose shapes seemed familiar. But unlike the original pigments, my so-called 'waterproof' inks had not survived this blink of time. The pebbles were blank. That is, all except for two. Both had lost their painted motif. But one rhomboid flattened shape was still faintly marked with the word 'wheel', and another, pointed and pyramid-shaped, ghosted the first few letters of the word 'share'. Appropriate words, I felt. The wheel of time. The need to share memory and knowledge if it is not to be eroded.

The next day I crossed the Minch and headed east. Close to home in the heartlands of Perthshire, I drove the length of Loch Tay. This valley hosts one of the richest concentrations of prehistoric rock carvings, particularly on the foothills of the Ben Lawers range rising over my left shoulder to nearly 4,000 feet, its highest summit marked by a great slab of quartz. The main rocks of these hills are mica schist and the denser epidiorite, but both are liberally veined with milky quartz, a variety made translucent by tiny bubbles of salty water and gas – relics of the hot fluid from which the vein minerals crystallised.

At home I realised that, as a walker, I've been on the trail of quartz for a long time. Small chips of it that I don't recall collecting tinkle out of pockets and it gleams out of the small piles of pebbles that end up on windowsills around my house. I'm drawn to those sparks of bright white on a path ahead or forming high and distinct waymarks and can recall walking with a piece clutched in my hand just for the pleasure of carrying it. The childish thrill of discovering it in a mountain pool or on the beach is like seizing natural treasure, redolent of gems, luck and rarity, which is ironic, as it is the most common mineral on Earth.

Quartz rings with magic across the world and back into antiquity. Caches of it are associated with Neolithic sites such as the sparkling facade of Newgrange passage tomb in Ireland. Within living memory I have heard of quartz chips left on graves in Argyll, or as a token when passing St Finnan's Well on the pass between Stontian and Polloch in the West Highlands. In many cultures of the world it is accredited with animistic powers.

It has more prosaic uses, too. Some varieties are of gem quality and quartz sand is used to make glass. Optical-grade crystals can be used as lenses. But it is the connection with timekeeping that we all know after Jacques and Pierre Curie proved in 1880 that squeezing quartz crystals produced piezoelectricity. Timers and electronic circuits followed, although most now use manufactured crystals.

It wasn't far off midwinter when I climbed out of the deeply frozen valley up onto the slopes of Ben Lawers. It was a 'Quartz day'. Every leaf and blade of grass was feathered in ice crystals. My feet crunched through puddles, and icicles hung in rows from the banks of burns waiting to be played like xylophones. Small waterfalls, where shaded, were fashioned into gnarled white grottoes, the boulders cased with ice, pools dotted with quartz pebbles. Sometimes when I saw a sheep's print filled with white sparkle I wasn't immediately sure whether it was ice or quartz. There is a natural association between the two. The word for 'crystal' comes from 'ice' in Greek, and Pliny the Elder believed quartz to be permanently frozen ice. Hand-coolers made from quartz were used through many centuries right up until Victorian times, when egg-shaped smooth pebbles soothed the palms of ladies afraid of offering a sweaty handshake.

But my favourite etymology is in the Irish. Quartz is *griancloch*, meaning 'sun rock'. As I walked steeply upwards from the shores of Loch Tay, I understood why. Despite the iron-hard white place below and crisp snow high above, I was in between in a strata of colour – a blaze of russet bracken, tawny grasses and luminous moss. The low sun scudding over the hills to the south of the Loch felt surprisingly warm and visually it sent a thrill through the veins of quartz writhing through rocks.

In knobbles, seams, knots, it stood proud of rock surfaces and brought a visceral memory of my rock-climbing days: how, on a featureless slab, I might have squeezed my fingers around one of these, or wedged a foot on it and felt joyously safe. Quartz is a survivor, withstanding the erosion of softer rock around it so that it almost appears like a jewel in a more mundane setting, in this case, one intricately laced with beautiful but less glitzy lichens. It is the same process that leaves quartzite – the 'sugary' sandstone made up of quartz grains – topping hills like the Grey Corries near Fort William, which can appear permanently snow-capped.

Ben Lawers means 'hill of loud water' and it earns its name. Numerous burns plummet from the tops of this range, dividing the land laterally into segments so that none of the paths traverse the hill; they climb and descend.

Close to the pounding of a waterfall, I found my first cup mark, a depression highlighted by the low-angled sun. I sank my fingers into it. Found more such marks. At the base of the rock a mole had been working, its archaeology unearthing from the dark soil some small chips and flakes of quartz. One of them had a sharpened, stylus-like point and as an experiment I swivelled it on another rock, easily making a mark, and penetrating more quickly if I used a larger stone to hammer it.

Thought to date from 4000 to 2000 BC, rock art in its simplest form is such cup-marking – small dish-shaped depressions made by pecking at the rock surface with a stone implement. Sometimes they appear in elaborate groups with concentric rings and channels. Like the decorated pebbles, the purpose of these carvings is gloriously mysterious. Are they maps, constellation diagrams, doodles by bored shepherds, graffiti? One thing is certain: quartz was used to make these marks.

A series of excavations between 2007 and 2010 around some of these carved stones has shed new light on the significance, not only of the carvings themselves but the materials used to make them, their location and the event of their making. Archaeologists Richard Bradley and Aaron Watson noted that carvings often accumulate close to the sight or sound of a waterfall, in the most sheltered spots of the hillside, and below the highest peaks. Pollen samples indicate that this was an open landscape much as it is now and the carvings would have been seen from significant viewpoints. Because they are nearly all on south-facing slopes, the designs would have been highlighted at particular times by both the sun and moon, seen travelling across the sky and reflected in the fifteen-mile length of Loch Tay below. It all suggests a special relationship to place.

Quartz was the tool, but the way it was deliberately left around the carved rocks suggests that it was not only chosen for its hardness and practical properties. Perhaps in the thinking of animistic society, the image remaining on the rock was powerful partly because of what was used to make it. For comparison, the archaeologists excavated around the base of two rocks in the area which had not been carved. They made no finds at these, whereas the carved ones presented artefacts, some on the top of the rocks and others at their base. Included were two pieces of pitchstone from Arran, worked flint, a quartzite pebble from a beach, possibly on the west coast, and a substantial quantity of broken and flaked quartz, probably collected as pebbles in nearby streams.

Contouring the hillside at around 15,000 feet, I spent the afternoon wandering between natural basins as if through a series of rooms. Most contained remnants of sheilings, simple buildings remembered now in tumbled stone where women and children stayed in the summer months, bringing the cattle for the high grazing. If I paused and closed my eyes on this still, un-peopled day, I soon conjured voices; voices associated with games and stories and cheese-making. These are the same places – sheltered, perched above a steep drop to the loch – where rock carvings from a much earlier people are found.

In my own 'pecking' experiments, I noted the high-pitched 'music' of quartz on quartz. Might this have echoed around these enclosed hollows in the hillside and made Ben Lawers 'the loud one' in more than one way? Even more exciting was the thought that friction might have generated quartz's special electricity. How potent a spectacle this would be if carvers at work glowed with triboluminescence – a phenomenon I had read about, but could barely believe. In Kilmartin, Argyll, platforms have been found close to carved rocks, possibly to accommodate an audience. They were covered in quartz. Might rock art have been partly about a performance?

A shamanistic connection between rock art and quartz might be hard for us to grasp with our twenty-first century rational minds and with the Enlightenment behind us. But like a slim mineral seam, I still sense it in my wish to hold and to collect quartz; a privilege I don't completely understand. The energy between the hand, quartz, sun, and vigorous water flow is unmistakable and in the depths of winter it fills me with hope, propels me towards lengthening days.

Back at home in the town, I slipped out into my dark garden with two pieces of quartz. It was an experiment I undertook sceptically. I rubbed them together, struck them off each other, and felt a surge of wintery pleasure as they illuminated my hands. I was a child with her first sparkler. I held a stone of light. I have held back from saying it directly, but this made me sure: quartz is a magic stone.

Caves

GREENLAND

Gina Moseley

A vast lake stretches out before me. It is long and narrow, bounded by dark limestone hills that rise sharply from its shores. In the distance, glaciers that have slowly crept down from the highest peaks glisten in the sun, while immediately in front of me, a bitterly cold breeze gently breaks the icy grey waters at my feet.

'You're in the Arctic now.'

It's a phrase that we have heard several times over the last few days. We don't feel like we're in the Arctic though. Greenland is the world's largest island, with four fifths of it covered by ice, but we're not confronted by vast snow-covered lands, dogs pulling sledges, or the dancing lights of the aurora borealis. Instead, grey clouds roll over this rocky, bare, grey-brown land, it's drizzling slightly, and there are no people.

We're in the ice-free land of Kronprins Christian Land in north-east Greenland. It's so far north that it's underneath the little plastic disc on the top of any classroom globe. The journey here has been long: eight years since I first had the idea, twenty-two months since I sent the first email, and four days of travelling and preparation since we left home. The Twin Otter that flew us along the east coast over ice sheets and icebergs disappears into the miserable grey clouds, first out of sight, then out of sound. This is when the five of us in our small expedition team realise we really are alone. The only sound now is the flapping of the Danish flag flying proudly next to us. I'm pleased it's flying; it means there is wind, and this means no mosquitoes.

The scientists who visited here twenty years ago reported no problems with mosquitoes. After three days of being here, I have 223 bites on my left arm alone. It is a sign that the region is changing. A sign that it is warming up. And that is the reason we are here.

In the 1950s and 1960s, geologists came for quite different reasons. They were accompanying the US Army and during the height of the Cold War, looking for ice-free landing sites in the Arctic. The old Nissen hut, sand-covered rowing boats, and big, blue heavy-duty water pump are a permanent reminder of their presence.

We're heading for 80.4 degrees north. There's not much land left after that, and the majority of the 7.3 billion people on this planet will be south of us. Specifically, we're heading to caves found in 440 million-year-old limestone.

These are some of the most northerly caves on the planet, and their existence has come as something of a surprise to my caving friends and palaeoclimate colleagues. They were somewhat of a surprise to me, when I found reference to their existence buried deep within the US caving literature. This refers to the caves as being on three levels, up to 40 feet wide and 200 feet long. From a sport or exploratory caving perspective they offer little interest. They're short and hard to reach. However, one sentence jumped out of that original manuscript that would change the fate of those caves and our interest in them forever. It read: 'The fill is capped by a flowstone deposit four inches thick formed of coarsely crystalline calcite.'

Perhaps that doesn't sound very exciting, but to me, as a palaeoclimate researcher, the excitement and significance of finding flowstone in north-east Greenland is unimaginable. If you've ever visited a cave, chances are you've seen flowstone. It is a calcite deposit like stalactites and stalagmites, except, instead of forming from dripping water, it is laid down in thin sheets by flowing water. That water has travelled from the oceans, through the atmosphere, soil and rock, before flowing through the deep, dark world beneath our feet. On its travels, the chemistry of the water is affected by the climate and environmental conditions through which it passes. In turn, as the water slowly deposits thin sheets of calcite in the cave, a distinct chemical signature is locked into it, creating an archive of the climate and environment during times long past.

Our mission is to collect a sample of the flowstone described in 1960. We want to unlock its secrets and find out what it can tell us about the past climate of the Arctic. We expect it will be much older than the current limit of the Greenland ice cores, which at the moment cover the last 123,000 years. Our results should provide us with completely new knowledge about the past climate in Greenland. We also expect it will be from a time that was warmer and wetter than today, and hence can be considered an analogue for how this region will develop in the future in a warmer world.

Our route to the caves will be long and arduous. During the preparations for this expedition, I spoke to several Arctic experts and people who had been here before. Unanimously, they were confident that we would not see any polar bears. They considered it too far inland, and there would be little if anything for them to eat. Yet in front of me by the rippling waters of the lake, near the Nissen hut and the flag pole, propped up against the mountain of aviation fuel drums, lie the remains of a magnificent but very dead polar bear. The organs and tissues have long since decayed. Only the skeleton remains upon a thick bed of white fur. The mouth is slightly open, exposing large canines among the set of forty-two teeth. Instinctively I knelt down and stroked the top of its head. It was slightly rough to the touch. My hand tiny against its massive skull. It brought a tear to my eye and a lump to my throat. This isn't how I imagined my first interaction with a polar bear to be.

We begin preparations to cross the lake, which, according to the satellite images, only became ice-free the week before. We launch, excited and eager to start the next part of the adventure. The feeling is short-lived. The river's too shallow, and now we look closer, we see that every few minutes, a huge chunk of the sandy spit of land crashes down into the water. My colleague Mark, who is the only person with waders, jumps in and pulls the boat back into deeper water. But we keep beaching because the weight of the boat and its load is too much for one person. There's nothing for it. Robbie and I take our boots and socks off and jump into the water.

After a while my toes are so cold I can't feel them. I'm worried. I've been to hospital with hypothermia before, and have long suffered from Raynaud's, the syndrome that numbs fingers and toes and turns them white. Our remoteness means we simply can't afford to let the situation develop further. We decide to drag the boat back to shore and rest the night hours in the ruined Nissen hut. After recharging on tea, powdered soup and our first taste of freeze-dried spaghetti bolognese, we turn our attention to the ease with which a polar bear could slice through the old sand-coloured canvas of our tent. We erect a bear fence made from thin orange polypropylene rope and a personal attack alarm. It should wake us in the event of an unwanted visitor, and maybe even scare them off, but it is a bit of a psychological game: I didn't sleep well.

The next morning, we try the river on the other side of the spit of land. It is a much better plan and we cross the lake without any further problems. The remainder of the journey to the caves is on foot. We have so much equipment and food to take with us that it is necessary to do it in shuttle runs.

Vandredalen is a classic, glacially formed, flat-bottomed U-shaped valley. It is wide. Really wide. I was told before that this is 'big country'. It couldn't have been truer. The distances seem limitless. No longer host to a large mass of ice, today the base of the valley is being reworked by the aqua-marine blue waters of the river that drains the lake.

Thanks to the mighty glaciers that have carved out this landscape, the terrain under foot isn't too difficult. At the moment, we're walking on a flat, elevated terrace of reddish-brown Neoproterozoic sandstones that were deposited anything between 700 million and 1.4 billion years ago. We wind through erratic boulders dotted on top of the sandstone, some the size of cars, made up of a conglomerate of red, beige and brown rocks cemented together in a chaotic colourful mess. Tall, steep, multicoloured scree slopes pour down from the imposing carbonate cliffs to our left, occasionally giving way to a small trickle of water, winding its way down from the ice cap to the isolated lakes in the valley bottom.

As we leave Vandredalen and enter Grottedalen, which means 'cave valley', the ground turns to a spongy, polygon-patterned soil. Pentagons, hexagons, heptagons. This is typical in permafrost environments, the result of the annual freeze-thaw of the active surface layer. The polygon path leads us all the way to the caves, but by the time we reach them the weight of the rucksack is taking its toll. I've been carrying half my own body weight for the last three days and the rest stops are becoming more frequent. The experience is made worse by our walking straight past the caves. We even see them and stop and comment. But Robbie and I are so convinced that the caves are in another valley that we carry on. I just have to swallow my embarrassment and shame for getting it wrong.

From the river, steep scree slopes rise up to vertical walls containing the caves. The twenty-four-hour sun swings round above our heads in a circle, dipping later in the day but never quite reaching the horizon. In full sun, the east wall containing the caves lights up in a beautiful warm orange glow, but this passes quickly, and the majority of the day is spent in bitterly cold shadow.

We know the highest-level caves have not been visited before. Access to them was previously considered too dangerous, but with my expert team of cave explorers, the five of us gain access to a small part of the world that no one else has ever seen before. It is a cliché, but yes, more people have been to the moon than some of those little caves deep within the Arctic Circle.

We start with the caves that are easiest to access. Lying on my stomach, crawling into a stone tube reveals the first calcite sample. It's a slim slither about 5 millimetres thick encrusting some broken limestone. It's a small but significant step. It means there might be other samples besides the one written about in 1960. We are not disappointed, and are soon excited to realise there is so much flowstone lying about, in both large and small caves, in situ and ex situ, that we don't know what to do with it. It is present in thin slithers on walls, thick sequences in notches, as large boulders to sit on, and in one cave as a bridge across a passage. In many instances, several-metre-thick sequences are intact on the surface – the caves that once sheltered them long since gone. It is better than we could ever have expected. We might well have gone to all this effort and found nothing. Instead, there is so much material we simply can't sample it all. We are under-resourced and this crushes our excitement a little. We decide to sample a broad range of material. It was always meant to be a pilot study, so if we can get a good idea of the material available to us, we might be able to build on that and return in the future.

One cave in particular was a highlight. It is high up in the valley wall with a fantastic view over Grottedalen. The entrance is a large oval, wider than it is high, and by Greenland standards is one of the longest at 40 metres. I'm preoccupied by a large flowstone deposit that we have found in the entrance: good-quality, dense, compact calcite. The guys disappear into a black space at the top of the sediment slope and call me up to join them. I don't have to get too close before I feel the bitter coldness of what lies beyond. Stalagmites 15 centimetres high, made out of clear and white ice, rise up from the floor. I carefully pick my way over them, eager not to dirty them. The black hole opens up into a chamber, about 1.5 metres high and 6 metres long. The only words escaping anyone's mouth are 'Wow!' Ice crystals as big as squash balls shimmer like chandeliers in the ceiling and on the walls. It is -6°C, though, so time to appreciate them is limited.

As we head down to the cave described in 1960 with the flowstone, my eye is caught by a small yellow piece of cardboard stored underneath the rocks. It looks like litter, so I reach through a gap to pick it up and take it out with me. Surprisingly, it turns out to be a Kodak film box. It's in excellent condition, sprinkled a little in some fine-grained, light-grey cave mud, but otherwise undamaged. Even the corners and edges show no signs of wear. The text reads 'Kodak X-PAN fast black and white film'. I play a game of guess-the-develop-before-date with Mark, Robbie and Chris. A range of answers come back, but all are far off. 'Dec 1961' can just be made out in faint grey print on the outside of the box. The box is yet to reveal its biggest secret though. Inside I find a foil bag encased in cream paper with 'Kodak' written in red lettering. Inside it, like reaching the final layer of a Russian doll, I find one page of blue lined paper ripped from a notebook. Curly writing in pencil covers half the page. The top right is dated June 29, 1930, followed by the statement that 'Walter H Memphis, Richard A Pirelli, Wm E Davies, AFCRC, US army and US Geological Survey visited here'. I never expected to experience this direct connection to the original explorers. The note raises some questions, though. Our understanding from the literature is that these caves were discovered in 1960, yet the writing clearly says 1930. It is a mystery that we just cannot answer.

The end of the expedition brings a deep sadness. It is an anticlimax. So much physical, emotional and mental effort has gone into this project over the last couple of years, culminating in just three days at the caves, which is now drawing to a close. Beside a few hiccups, which only added to the excitement and adventure, the whole thing has gone better than expected. It is a huge relief not only to have a bag full of samples, but more importantly, everyone is going home unharmed and in full health, though perhaps weighing slightly less than when we started. It was worth coming. The reality turned out to be better than the dream. And now onto the next chapter. Months of lab work lie ahead. It is an exciting but daunting prospect. There is still a chance the samples will be unsuitable for analysis and this is an unsettling thought, but after all – that is the nature of research.

Fall of the Wild

ALASKA

Jason Mark

Finally, I discovered the uninterrupted wild I had been searching for – though I had to travel to one of the farthest ends of Earth to find it.

For five days we had paddled the Aichilik River through the Arctic National Wildlife Refuge, the fabled wilderness on the north slope of Alaska's Brooks Range that, for some twenty years, has been the site of a long-running battle between the oil corporations that want to drill there and the environmental groups and native tribes that are opposed to any fossil-fuel development. Now, we were at the shores of the Arctic Ocean. After a few of us took a plunge into the ice-filled waters (having come all this way, why not?), the group settled in for the everlasting evening. Almost everyone had gone to sleep, but I decided to stay up, determined to catch every last minute at the top of the globe.

The stillness was flawless. There was no wind – nor leaf or grass for wind to stir, anyway – and the water was perfectly flat, unblemished, like a plate of brass. As the sun made a lazy arc through the northern sky the temperature dropped to around 6°C, sending a fog off the ocean. The light turned thick as honey; sea and sky fused into a single field of orange. An immense silence descended. Now and again I could hear the muffled boom of an ice sheet collapsing off in the distance, the wingbeats of eider flocks zipping among the ice floes.

I would call the scene all pristine – but I know better. Ethereal was more like it. Otherwordly. Here remained a place where one could escape the sights and sounds of civilisation. And here, too, was a place large enough and remote enough for evolution to rule. The Arctic, at least, remained the wild of the imagination.

And yet. The things we had experienced during our trip down the Aichilik had only deepened my doubts about the future of wildness. The tundra was untamed, but it was not untouched. Even in such a remote place, humanity's thumb pressed firmly on the scale. We were about as far as you can get from civilisation, yet the environmental impacts of human technology on the landscape – climate change, especially – were obvious.

Worrisome new questions had arisen in my mind during the course of our group's float down the river. In this Human Age, the Anthropocene – with the force and speed of our technologies causing unprecedented ecosystem damages – was it still worthwhile to try and keep some places wild? Especially if such a hands-off approach might doom plants and animals to extinction? Don't we have a responsibility to make an effort to repair the damage we are causing, though that would likely mean trammelling the wilderness?

The thought was disturbing: in a time of environmental hardship, maybe the wilderness has become a luxury. If we want to help nonhuman nature survive the global fever we've created, we might have no choice but to bring wild landscapes further under human control. To 'save nature', will we have to sacrifice wilderness?

We had started from Fairbanks a week earlier. It was only a couple of days after the summer solstice, and as we drove from our hotel to the Fairbanks airport for a 7 am takeoff, the light was already full, as if it were closer to noon. We lifted off, made a turn over Fairbanks, headed northwards. The planes passed over a line of silver zigzagging through the green woods – the Trans-Alaska Pipeline, pumping crude down from the Prudhoe Bay oil fields. For a while we could spot cabins and the occasional gravel road. And then there was nothing but the vast sweep of the bush. Hills after hills, dotted with the cones of spruce trees and countless nameless ponds. About ninety minutes north of Fairbanks we flew over the broad Yukon River and entered the mountains. That's when the importance of visibility became apparent. We wouldn't be flying over the mountains – we would be flying through them.

After the last spruce and the final fir faded away, the landscape emptied out even more. The mountains were stripped to their essentials: rock ribboned with water, green slopes of grasses and moss, and little else. The terrain was a work in progress. I remembered that the Arctic is one of the youngest ecosystems on Earth. Just yesterday (geologically speaking), the region was covered in thick sheets of ice, and so it has had little chance to develop. The deep freeze of the long winters slows down time further; it can take fifty years for a tree to grow to five feet. The empty valleys looked half-formed, as if Creation had been suspended halfway through Day Three.

Even sitting in the plane's rear seats, it was clear we were having trouble. We headed into a mountain valley only to find the end enclosed by clouds. Suddenly Daniel, the pilot, made a sharp U-turn. A cliff face spun past the wingtip, the sharp peaks whirling just beyond our little cockpit.

We probed a second valley, but again hit a wall of clouds and had to make another nail-biting reversal. Incredibly, Daniel was navigating from memory. An Alaska Native, Daniel had grown up in a cabin north of the Yukon River, and he knew the mountain range as well as I know the streets and alleys of San Francisco. But he couldn't find a way through. The passes were all closed.

After one more futile attempt to find a gap through the clouds, we made a beeline back southwards, headed for Arctic Village, a hamlet situated at 68 degrees north that is home to an Alaska Native people called the Gwich'in. Stopping in Arctic Village hadn't been on our itinerary, but until the clouds cleared we would have no choice but to wait there.

The Gwich'in's traditional lands stretch from Fort McPherson in Canada's Northwest Territories across the US border to the east and north of the Yukon River, and Arctic Village (or Vashr....I K'......in their language) is one of the nation's older settlements. A scant two hundred people live there. The houses are mostly US-government-issued prefab cottages painted a cheerful array of colours. 'Downtown,' as I heard one local refer to the crossroads at the centre of the village, consists of a one-room grocery, a dilapidated Episcopalian church, the offices of the Gwich'in Steering Committee, and a sparkling new US post office and elementary school. Beyond that there's no sign of civilisation, only a vastness of forest, lakes and mountains.

After we landed on the gravel airstrip at the edge of the village, some of the Gwich'in got us set up in their community hall to wait out the rain. Our main host was Sarah James, a longtime member of the Gwich'in Steering Committee and one of the most vocal opponents of oil drilling in the refuge's coastal plan. Round-faced, with long, silver hair, James zipped around the village on her All Terrain Vehicle, to enlist her nephews in making sure that we had fresh water and firewood for the stove.

The Gwich'in are famous for being uncompromising about their sovereignty, and the tribe's spirit of resistance was on display there in the community hall. Protest banners hung from the walls of the log building. 'Save the Earth,' declared one that sported the iconic NASA photograph of our planet from space. 'Save Gwich'in Way of Life,' another read, and below that, 'Our culture is not for sale. Support .. Wilderness.'

The Gwich'in's commitment to the inviolability of their territory holds strong today. In the 1990s and early 2000s, Republicans in Washington pushed to open up part of the Arctic National Wildlife Refuge to oil drilling. Naturally, the Sierra Club and other conservation groups fought back. In that fight, the Gwich'in provided key moral leadership. They said the refuge should be given permanent wilderness protection, and they warned that drilling would disrupt or destroy the calving grounds of the caribou herds that tribal members still depended on for a significant amount of their protein.

The day faded to the sprawling, hours-long dusk that is an Arctic summer night. We were invited to Sarah's brother Gideon's cabin for moose stew. As happens among strangers, the talk turned to the weather. Gideon and Sarah agreed that all of the rain in the middle of summer was odd. 'It's too warm, and it's too wet,' Sarah said. 'It didn't used to rain like this in the summer time.' The rainy summers were just one of many changes in the weather that the brother and sister had witnessed. Gideon said, 'It's a lot warmer. It don't get that cold no more in the winter time. We used to get ice that thick' – and with his hands he measured out about four feet of length. 'Now it's just barely that thick,' and he cut the distance in half.

The changes wrought by global warming are happening right outside Gideon James's front door, and he expressed frustration that the question of whether humans are causing the problem remains a matter of political debate. 'It's happening, though,' Gideon said. 'It's happening because the weather never cools off. It's dangerous. It's scary. Some people, they don't understand. Just like some of our state legislators don't believe it. Some of our leaders don't believe it. Some of these people who don't believe it, they got kids. They got grandkids. They need to think twice about it. But big-money people like millionaires, they go and lobby them and they believe them.' Gideon said, 'This Earth is not balanced no more. It's like this,' and he tilted his hands at a forty-five-degree angle.

Gideon James is right, of course. The science is unequivocal: the planet is warming, and human activities are to blame. Since the start of the Industrial Revolution and the beginning of fossil-fuel burning, atmospheric concentrations of carbon dioxide have increased from 280 parts per million to more than 400 ppm today, the highest level in about 650,000 years. Meanwhile, the Arctic has warmed disproportionately fast, between 2° and 4°C. This is largely because of the historically unprecedented melting of Arctic sea ice, which has changed the region's albedo – that is, its reflectivity of the sun's heat and light. While white ice reflects heat, a dark ocean absorbs it. The steady diminishment of sea ice makes the region warmer, and in the process creates a feedback loop in which even more warming occurs.

Global warming is obvious in Alaska today. Permafrost is no longer so permanent, and as the ground melts, roads and power lines across the state are beginning to buckle and twist. A bark-beetle infestation has hammered the state's conifer forests, since warmer winters and longer summers allow the beetles to reproduce more easily. As the forests die, wildfires (always a force on the landscape) have become more intense. Berries and trees are moving northwards. Migratory birds such as sandpipers and phalaropes are nesting up to a week earlier. Polar bears have moved inland and mated with grizzly bears, creating a new hybrid animal dubbed the 'pizzly bear'.

In the Arctic, geology and biology are star-crossed. Beneath the land lie huge deposits of oil and gas. And were those resources to be tapped, the landscape and its life forms would be radically transformed, thanks to climate change's disproportionate effects on the Far North.

The ironies of the Arctic also involve a patent injustice for the few people that live there. The communities that have done the least to cause climate change are the ones experiencing its impacts most harshly. At least three native towns – the Inupiaq villages of Kivalina and Shishmaref, and the Yup'ik village of Newtok – likely will have to be abandoned and their residents relocated owing to coastal erosion and increased flooding connected to rising seas.

Even the most remote regions are entangled with civilisation, as the Gwich'in know all too well. 'If you have polluted air, it doesn't go up into space and just go away. It stays here with us,' Gideon said as we ate our moose stew. 'When I worked for the tribe, I travelled down to the lower forty-eight states many times. I saw those goddamn eight-lane and sixteen-lane freeways going with cars twenty-four hours a day. All of that carbon dioxide, where does it go? It doesn't go nowhere. It stays right here with us.'

He paused for a moment, embarrassed to be preaching, and said apologetically: 'I get carried away talking about this stuff. I don't care if someone believes a different way. I don't care. But I know what I'm talking about.'

'I know this husband and wife,' Sarah told me, as we did the dishes. 'They are out there in the bush all the time hunting and fishing, and they know the land and everything, but she went right into the river on a snow machine when the ice was too thin. Because things are changing. The knowledge that we've had for thousands of years is somehow changing. We have to relearn what's going on in order to tell our people which way is safe.'

To use, or not to use? That is the question posed by wilderness today. The oil and gas companies say: 'Use it.' Environmentalists and their Indigenous allies say: 'No.' Sarah James told me that before the arrival of the whites, the Gwich'in had no word for 'wilderness'. Indeed, this is the case for most hunter-gatherer societies, for whom there is no sharp dividing line between the domesticated and the wild. During an unprecedented summit nearly thirty years ago of all the tribe's members to discuss the fate of the refuge, the elders took time out to come up with a

Gwich'in expression synonymous with the word 'wilderness'. 'It took them a long time,' James said. They finally settled on the phrase, *The place where life begins*. 'Leave it the way the Creator made it,' she told me. 'That way we will know it is protected.'

The question is not just to drill or not to drill, but whether any place can remain as 'the Creator made it' and still be 'protected'.

Slate

ERYRI (SNOWDONIA)

Gillian Clarke

It is almost Christmas, and we have come to spend the holiday at my maternal grandparents' farm in north-east Wales, between the River Dee and the Berwyn hills. In the big farm kitchen, my Taid smokes his pipe in the wing chair on the right-hand side of the range. In the scullery across the passage my Nain is plucking the goose. She stands in a blizzard of feathers falling onto the huge slate slabs of the floor. My mother's youngest sister, Elen, sweeps them into a drift in the corner to gather and save for pillows and feather beds. Then she fills a tin pail at the sink, and flings a wave of soapy water over the slate floor. It darkens to purple. The suds are swept out of the door, down the passage, into the yard, and the floor dries slowly to lavender.

Slate is our stone, from the quarries of Snowdonia, just as the coal in the grate is ours, from the South Wales coalfield. We tread on slate every day. Penrhyn slate, from Bethesda, Snowdon, Eryri, mount of eagles. It floors the *beudy*, too, where the cows sway home, clattering and slipping on the stones morning and evening, each to her own stall, for milking. Next to the scullery is the dairy. The dairy slab is a huge, unbroken slice of mountain. Like the dairy and larder slabs in all the neighbouring farms, it is ice-cold, and it keeps cool the churns, jugs and bowls of milk, their cream rising, and a pat of butter fresh from churning and printed with a sheaf of wheat, and the cold corpse of the goose-fleshy goose, plucked, stuffed and trussed for the oven.

In 1819, my young paternal great-grandfather was working the stone boats, loading slate from Caernarfon dock for the crossing to Anglesey. By the end of the nineteenth century, Penrhyn, one of many slate quarries in Snowdonia, was the world's largest, worked by nearly three thousand quarrymen. Slate sills, thresholds, floors, larder slabs, gravestones. Slabs wired as uprights for fences; two vertical and one horizontal for a stile; massive orthostats for gateposts; odd shapes set flat for a path from door to washing line. A tilted slab under brambles and leaning trees in a derelict chapel graveyard is engraved with the names of my maternal great-grandparents. Then another stone, a clean slate slab upright in sunlight in mown grass, where my Nain and Taid are remembered, he coming in from the yard, stamping on the threshold like a horse, she in the scullery, plucking, plucking.

In city, town, village and upland farm, we sleep under Welsh slate. Rain sings on it. It has roofed every house I have ever lived in. It helped power the Industrial Revolution. It roofs the terraced houses of much of Britain, draws the contour lines of valleys, delineating the curved streets of pit-villages climbing the mountain slopes.

Despite our twice-yearly family visits from Cardiff to visit Nain on the farm in Denbighshire – Taid died when I was three – I had never experienced the north-western mountains of Snowdonia until my father, a first-language Welsh-speaker and passionate Welshman, decided I should know the beauty and infinite variety of my country's landscape as well as its culture and its industrial history. When I was twelve he took me on a long drive north through Snowdonia. It was on that journey that I first saw the spectacular slate-tips and quarries of Blaenau Ffestiniog and Bethesda, and some of the great waterfalls of the north. It was like first experiencing Cubism after studying nineteenth-century landscape painting. The familiar earth had been taken apart, and its components, stone, water, weather, light, had been re-formed by a giant creator. It was, indeed, a terrible beauty. To this day the sight of slate-tips in rain never fails to fill me with awe, such an unbearable weight of angles and shards, of greys, purples, silvers, broken pieces of sky, so many deaths, so much lost life. So much geological and human history.

Eryri – mount of eagles – is Snowdon's true name. The eagles have gone, but we walk the mountain under the floating shadows of peregrine, chough, ring ouzel, hen harrier, merlin. The first time I climbed Snowdon was on a rare fine day, the sun on our backs as we leaned to the slope, foot after foot, heaving our way to the summit, concentrating on the track beneath our feet, shale worn grassless by boot and hoof. Sometimes, needing to draw breath, needing to look, we paused, stood still and turned to the view. Was it that time – I can't be sure – that beyond unfolding peak after peak, there, stretched out before me lay England, or at least the Cheshire plain, reaching eastwards in a golden haze, with Wales all around me, and to the west the misty blues of the Irish Sea. Once, roughly following the train-track down, I witnessed what is called a 'glory', an unbroken circular rainbow below in the mist of the Llanberis Pass. There the path runs vertiginously close to the edge, and below is nothing but the sheer drop of the mountain. Another time, after climbing for hours in rain, I saw skies clear to reveal a world as simple as a map, from the misty distances of England to the mirage of Ireland, and Anglesey – Môn, mother of Wales – as if in a school atlas.

Alongside the track, in the grass, on slopes and in crevices, is beauty in miniature. Sometimes I have known the name of a tiny flower growing there, often not, though there are botanical treasures, mountain flowers growing in Arctic scree, in grains and dusts of sand, granite, quartzite, on precipice, crevice and grassy ledge, on the vertical rock walls of rivers and waterfalls: parsley fern, fir club-moss, woolly fringe moss, liverwort, wavy hair grass, sheep's fescue, foxglove, heath bedstraw, heather, bilberry, myrtle, and crevice communities of ferns, mosses, lichens, arctic saxifrage, maidenhair, spleenwort, liverwort, and the brittle blade fern.

Most special of all, unique to this place, in rocky clefts too steep for nibbling sheep, grows the Snowdon lily, a delicate white flower shivering in the wind. It has survived since the Ice Age on Snowdon's north-facing cliffs, the only Arctic-type rock-crevice conditions north of the Alps. It has evolved alone, a unique survivor. I have never seen it. I am content to imagine it, to believe in it, to relish its picture in the botanical guide, to enjoy its name, to feel proud that Edward Lhuyd listed the flora of Snowdon on a visit to the mountain in 1688, where he first identified this lovely flower, to be named after him: *Lloydia Serotina*.

There are special invertebrates, too. A few examples of a species of rainbow beetle, the genetically distinct *Chrysolina cerealis*, the Snowdon rainbow beetle, were trapped, like the Snowdon lily, after the last Ice Age. The creature survived to evolve alone on Snowdon's western flanks, on crags away from grazing sheep. It feeds on flowers of the wild thyme. Even its breakfast sounds romantic!

The climb takes all the energy of body and mind, and only the naturalist knows where to look for a tiny flower or a beetle. When you walk a mountain track, stepping up, up the shale paths, stopping to catch your breath, to gaze into rain, or mist, or sometimes across infinite space to far peaks and valleys rising at every upward step, the voids beneath your feet, and the dead who hollowed them, can be far from mind. One is the opposite of the other, as light is of the dark, as airy space is of claustrophobic enclosure. Yet the spent power of the pits and quarries has left behind volumes of emptiness, and water. The mountain strums with rivers, lakes and waterfalls, sings with streams: Glaslyn, Gorsen, Cwm Llan, Afon y Cwm. There are ruins of farms, the *hafod* (the shepherd's summer house) and the *hendre* (his winter house), the quarrymen's sleeping barracks, bridges and walls all made of slate and rubble and river stones. There are ghost-works rusting and rattling in the wind, dead streams blue with copper, deserted mine workings, cathedrals of emptiness where it is impossible to forget the people who lived briefly and died there.

Without subsistence farming there would not have been slate. Without slate, there would be no farms up here, in this windswept place. The ruins of both are the story. They came from the hill-farms of greater Snowdonia, or as far afield as Anglesey, leaving behind a bit of land to work, a large family to feed. Father and older brothers travelled here to work six days a week in the quarry or the mine, while mother and daughters cared for stock, and tilled a scrape of land.

> The mountain has secrets,
> tunnels into the seep and drip of the dark,
> into the stone womb, under roots of trees,
> past wheels, pulleys, chains, trucks locked
> in their pollens of rust.
>
> Deep as the Ordovician, old workings,
> mine-shafts, mullock heaps, piles of slag,
> abandoned two centuries back, river-stones
> stained blue with copper, copper-iron's gold,
> sulphates from the mountain's heart.
>
> Imagine the miner stoop under its porch,
> to the knees in ice where light dies at the brink.
> Darkness. Echoes. Bats hang like rags. A stream
> falls three hundred feet in glittering stillness,
> and ferns sip sunlight at a rock fissure.

Rungs crook rusted steps over the void,
the miner's footprint in air, his handprint on rock
slimed by centuries of rain. He and water
hollowed the mountain, the fallen stone
of his cry swallowed in centuries of silence.

Once, after a long climb in the company of poets, we stoop into the mountain past *No Entry*, *Perygl*, *Danger*, under a low portal in sheer rock. We follow an arrow of torchlight, stepping along rusted tramlines into a black tunnel, narrow and low at first, before space opens suddenly, vertiginously into the first gallery. We know the void without seeing anything but blackness. It is measured in the altered note of our breaths, heartbeats, voices. It hears our bodies' vibrations sounding a pit too vast for the beam of a torch to measure. It has its own sounds, too. There are cries and whispers out there, down there, across the void. Our eyes get used to the dark. First, a streak of gold light from the roof of the mine – a stream falling though a rock fissure, sleeved in fern, then water falling free through light into dark. Someone with a powerful flashlight sends a beam to touch the far wall. We make out hooks and rungs driven into the rock where miners climbed all day long, slept seven nights in slate barracks on the mountain, worked the face for six days, went home for Sunday chapel, a few family hours, then returned to work their youth and health away. Many fell from those hooks and rungs into the terrible void below. To oblivion. I imagine the curved sound diminishing into the depths where a man's cry drowns but never stops echoing.

Not just slate, but copper, and other metals and minerals were worked from these mountains, left hollow and haunted once the profits were made. The life of a falling miner was soon replaced from the endless queue of the jobless, trying to add to the income of subsistence farming. Departed profiteers leave nothing but ghosts behind.

Slate is slow in the making. It is the finest-grained of all rock. Foliated, metamorphic, formed in a furnace of low heat and pressure out of sedimentary shale that had already been laid down millions of years earlier as clay or volcanic ash. Thought of those ages makes me dizzy, eons of volcanic activity, the rise and fall of oceans, pressure of sedimentary leftovers, glaciers and their detritus. The mineral recipe is geology's music: quartz, muscovite, illite, biotite, chlorite, hematite, pyrite, sometimes apatite, graphite, kaolinite, magnetite, tourmaline, zircon, feldspar. Sometimes there are iron nuclei in Snowdonian slate, forming 'bubbles' of pale green in the purple. I step across such a threshold every day. Sometimes there are the remains of delicate organisms.

The foliation of slate can lie vertical to the direction of the compression. A skilled slate-cutter can split slates clean and flat and of a size ready for roofing, or thick ones for flooring, larger for gravestones, fences, stiles, a massive slab for a dairy or larder.

We have always found uses for the power of water inside or on the mountain. I think of the simple way they churned butter in my mother's home farm. Hand-churning butter is hard work, and there were ten children in the family. Opposite the farm door there was a gap in the wall over a fast-flowing stream. The churn was placed in the gap, and connected to a small water wheel turned by the current in the river below. Thus, every day, milk was churned to fresh butter. A few hundred yards downstream, the same millstream ground the corn to flour. The power of water is infinite and its uses multiple. It is never exhausted.

The rise and fall of demand, and storage of unused power, are still unsolved problems in the generation and use of electricity. We must generate for maximum demand, and waste the rest. One of Britain's most impressive electricity power stations is at the abandoned Dinorwic slate quarry, its machinery buried deep inside the mountain, Elidir Fawr. Water is stored high above in the

Marchlyn reservoir. At times of peak demand, the gates are opened and water is set free to pour down, down through the turbines into Llyn Peris. At night, times of low demand, the water is pumped back up into the reservoir, and held until needed. Power withheld. Its metaphor might be the two mythical dragons of Snowdon, whose final battle gave victory to the red dragon over the white. I think of that sleeping power when, on a clear day, I see the blue peak of Snowdon, unmistakable across the waters of Cardigan Bay.

Snowdon's main farm, Hafod y Llan, the mountain grazing, its rivers and lakes, are now run by the National Trust, saved from the mad, bad dreams of a developer with a hotel, power boats and lakeside development in mind. Instead, the mountain flock is cut to just one thousand sheep, the grazing and house are run organically, and the Trust has developed a new hydroelectricity scheme. A turbine beside broken walls in the copper-poisoned waters of Craflwyn, 'dead' blue-green waters where no fish live, now produces enough electricity for all the National Trust's houses in Wales. What has been ripped from the guts of the mountain, scattering the slopes with ruins and the bones of the dead, impoverished a tenant people and enriched distant landowners, has found a kind of resolution. Hafod y Llan is ours, and Eryri awaits the return of the eagles.

Red Sandstones
PORTISHEAD

Ronald Turnbull

New Red Sandstone

I'm sitting on a low, lumpy bit of sea cliff just south of Portishead, looking down the Bristol Channel. The cliff is pebbles and small boulders, in different colours and kinds, bound together with rust-coloured sand. It's part of the New Red Sandstone – so called because of being only 250 million years old.

The New Red starts off on the south Devon coast, where it forms fine sea stacks at Ladram Bay, and tall, rather collapsible cliffs at Budleigh Salterton. The next big blob northwards is in Northampton, then in Staffordshire. A ring around the Lake District gives the red cliffs at St Bees and the handsome red towns of Penrith and Carlisle. And in Dumfriesshire's Nith valley, I live not only on the New Red Sandstone but also in it: my two-hundred-year-old house was built by a quarry master out of the bedrock in my own back garden.

The New Red is a soft stone, which is pretty happy to turn back into the sand it is made out of. It forms gentle, fertile farmland where the green of the fields contrasts with the cheerful red of the rocks in the few places where it does appear.

But its main effect is on the human population: an irresistible urge to carve and shape it. Stonemasons supplied with New Red Sandstone make handsome red town houses; hence, too, in the New Red lands, a tendency to decorative excess in the making of gravestones. The wealthy tradesmen buried alongside Robert Burns in Dumfries have graves the size of four-poster beds, carved all over with their relations and their interesting achievements; it is the eighteenth-century version of a Facebook page.

In a field beside the River Nith stands the worn-down remnant of an Anglian cross, carved all over with birds and foliage. Beside it, the red stone of the eighteenth-century Nith Bridge glows in the low winter sun like the embers of a coal fire. Two fields up from the Saxon cross, stands one of the dry-stone cones by land artist Andy Goldsworthy. The flat, square chunks of the sandstone made the overhanging sides of this one a bit easier to build.

And it is not just us people that carve the red sandstone. A mile from my house, a land artist called the Linn Burn has been joining in with the fun. The stream is small enough to paddle across in wellington boots; but in the twenty thousand years since the Ice Age, it has carved down into the sandstone a hundred feet deep, curves and caves of red rock all green and spongy with liverwort and ferns.

In the bedrock below Nottingham and its red sandstone castle, there is a rabbit warren of cellars and secret passageways; by the time you've carved your cellar, you've got all the masonry for your upstairs. And if you're King Edward III, the sandstone passages are just right for sneaking in and snatching the treasonable Earl of March from inside the castle.

At Kinver Edge, in Staffordshire, the houses are not just made out of the New Red, but also into it. The early hermit carved himself a simple cave, door and two windows. But in the eighteenth century, they cut whole cottages out of the bedrock, fireplaces and chimneys, and now the National Trust offers tea and cream cakes inside a desert dune of 250 million years ago.

For early geologists, the New Red was one of the Universal Formations – the same rock, all over the place geographically, but always in the same place in the succession of the stones. On top of the New Red will be the Jurassic, with its ammonites, and on top of that, the chalk. Underneath the New Red would be the Carboniferous, with its coal. We now know that the New Red isn't actually everywhere: but it is in Greenland, Mexico, North America and parts of North Africa.

Mexico, Greenland, North America and us: the New Red is telling us that all these places were once side-by-side, huddled together in the centre of the world's one continent, which we now name as Pangaea. And the reason for its rusty colour is that at that time this clump of places was to be found around a thousand miles north of the Equator, in the dry climate zone that today holds the Gobi Desert and the Sahara.

In my quarry village back in Dumfriesshire, we have a geological joke about all this. Our red sandstone didn't only make the town hall of Glasgow: it was also loaded into ships and carried across to New York. When you look at the brownstones of New York, it is hard to tell which is the red sandstone of Scotland, and which is from nearby New Jersey. Because of course they are the same thing. Over 50 million years, as the Atlantic opened, the UK's New Red Sandstone moved away eastwards. Then they loaded it into boats and brought it back again...

The good building stone is made of desert sand; and in it you can see the crosswise diagonal patterns of successive sand dunes. Meanwhile, the crunching together of the Pangaea supercontinent had raised a great mountain range. Wadis carved into those mountains, and when the rains came, flash floods washed great fans of gravel and boulder out into the plains. One of those flash flood fans is the pebble-and-boulder stone I am sitting on here at Somerset's seaside.

Old Red Sandstone

Given the New Red Sandstone, there pretty well has to be an Old Red Sandstone; nearly twice as old, in fact, at around 400 million years. One huge slab of the Old Red forms the Brecon Beacons, 40 miles wide, 2,000 feet thick, right across South Wales. The great cliff looks north across the farmland, red and reddish-brown in level stripes as if drawn with a ruler by some fussy landscape designer. At the highest point of the line, Pen y Fan, the red slabs are rubbed bare by the feet of hillwalkers. I crossed them in rain and fading light, and in a somewhat dazed state – it was in the middle of an attempt to cross the whole of that long escarpment in a single non-stop journey. And on those slabs, underneath the rainwater, I saw the ripples left on a red sandbank, in a red sandy estuary, under the subtropical sun of 400 million years ago.

Up in the Black Isle of Easter Ross in 1820, a teenager called Hugh Miller had the same experience. Impoverished by the early death of his father, he took work as a humble quarryman. It was going to be tough, and hard on the hands: as a compensation, it would involve explosions and fun with gunpowder.

On his second day at work, the mass of rock loosened by the gunpowder was lifted away, exposing fresh bedrock underneath.

> The entire surface was ridged and furrowed, like a bank of sand that had been left by the tide an hour before … [just as] I had observed it a hundred and a hundred times, when sailing my little schooner in the shallows left by the ebb. But what had become of the waves that had thus fretted the solid rock? I felt as completely at fault as Robinson Crusoe did on his discovering the print of the man's foot on the sand.

Hugh Miller used his skills in turning Old Red Sandstone into roadside gravel to uncover most of the world's first fossil fish, and thus gain entry to the Edinburgh intelligentsia, where, in his homespun black-and-white blanket, he lectured the professors on the wonders of God's creation and the antediluvian mysteries in an incomprehensible Black Isle dialect known as North Northern Scots.

The desert dunes, flash floods and lake bottoms of Miller's Old Red lie under Exmoor, and much of the Scottish Lowlands. At Stonehaven it forms high cliffs and sea stacks. Inland is green and pleasant pasture, but the cliff is knobbed like buried bones and the colour of dried blood, and on it stands Dunnottar, the most grimly picturesque of Scotland's castles.

Orkney is a different place altogether – for the Orcadians, 'Scotland' means all the other parts of Scotland not including Orkney. After the antique and mangled rocks of the Highlands, Orkney is a well-behaved landscape that could be the meadows of Herefordshire. Except that eighty percent of it is not there: taken away by the sea. The air is free of the pollution that we southerners long ago stopped noticing like the dirt on our spectacles – and the unworldly light is doubled by the reflection of the sea that is just behind the low curve of the hill.

Timber here is a luxury, and fence wire is twisted between upright slabs of gritty red sandstone. Stone Age Man built those flat slabs into doorsteps and kitchen cabinets at Scara Brae; Hugh Miller split them to find his fishes. Below the low, slabby cliffs, the ever-anxious sea washes against oval stones striped pink and ochre like beachballs, as if the beachballs were in faded sepia photos of long ago.

Portishead

I said that underneath the New Red Sandstone, and on top of the Old Red, is the Carboniferous; and as I walked down the coast just now from the Portishead paddling pool, I was picking up bits of crinoid out of tropical shoreline of 300 million years ago. But over half a mile of coastline that coal-age chunk of crust dwindles to nothing; Portishead is one of the places where the New Red and the Old Red lie right up against each other. Here at Kilkenny Bay, we look at the Old Red and the New together, to compare the differences.

Except that there isn't any. At knee-level is the Old Red Sandstone, a nicely layered freestone; it would make a great gravestone. The top of the Old Red has been eroded away, and onto it comes a reddish-brown flash-flood jumble of the New Red. Both of them show desert dunes, cemented with red iron oxide somewhere hot and dry. And both of them are sometimes these rubbly flash-flood boulders, or an old lake bed floored with red sand. If we're lucky, in the Old Red we might find one of Hugh Miller's fossil fish – the stripy bit of cliff just back towards Portishead does have fish scales in it. If we're really lucky, in the New Red we might find some dinosaur footprints. But otherwise, they both look just the same.

When the New Red was formed we were down level with the Sahara. Going further back in time, 100 million years before we were at the level of the Sahara, we were at the same distance from the Equator to the south: the dry climate zone that now contains the Kalahari Desert and the Atacama of Peru.

As the UK was moving through that southern desert zone, it happened that there was another huge mountain range, the one formed when Scotland crashed into England. That range poured sand and rubble out across a great swathe of territory, known as the Old Red Sandstone Continent: the land that is now America, and Greenland, Norway, Siberia, Poland and Russia – and Scotland.

After the Old Red, the UK moved across the Equator: and next up, there comes a layer of tropical reefs and coal swamps – the Carboniferous. Here at Kilkenny Bay all that got eroded away before we moved into the northern desert zone and the upper layer of desert sands, the New Red Sandstone. (But even so, we can see the missing 100 million years in the tilt of the rocks. During those missing 100 million years, the supercontinent Pangaea was crashing together, raising that second great mountain range – and tilting the

Old Red Sandstone, currently down level with my knees, slantwise through about twenty degrees. While the New Red, which comes in on top afterwards, lies more or less level.)

The Great Dying

The Old Red occupies the geological period called the Devonian. The New Red spans two separate geological periods, which tend to get lumped together as the Permo-Triassic. Dunes and flash floods, flash floods and dunes – and given that dinosaurs don't hang around in the red desert because there's nothing to eat, the New Red isn't a great place for finding fossils.

But in other parts of the world, the Permian and Triassic layers do have fossils. Those fossils suddenly stop. All the coral in all the world's oceans: it stops. The trilobites: gone for ever. The giant amphibians that dominated the swamps and forests: virtually wiped out, leaving the field clear for those upstart dinosaurs. Out of every twenty species of living things, nineteen become extinct. It is quite a lot worse than the comet that hit us 190 million years later and wiped out the dinosaurs. It is called the Great Dying.

We don't know what caused this disaster, or quite how quickly it happened. Geologists suspect an outpouring of basalt lava, the Siberian Traps, now seen over 1,800 miles of northern Russia. The basalt lava will have released huge amounts of carbon dioxide; the result seems to have been a change in the climate, the winds and the oceans, which slowed down and even stopped the Earth's ocean currents – leaving most marine life to simply suffocate to death.

We don't know exactly what went wrong. However, measurement of the oxygen-18 isotope lets any physicist with a decent mass spectrograph determine the temperature of the sea at the time. The disaster caused – was caused by – was, anyway, associated with – a rise in temperature of 8°C.

The present aim of world governments is to limit the global warming caused by us people to 2°C – which is hopeless, as we have more or less got there already. If we really got our act together, we could probably level it off at 4°C. Which is only half-way to the disaster, whatever it was, that wiped the Earth almost clean of life 250 million years ago.

And yet, somewhere between here in Somerset and my home in Dumfriesshire, that worldwide disaster fits into the space between two grains of sand. On Portishead foreshore, I'm about to step down from the red stone of the dinosaur time – back 150 million years into the time of Hugh Miller's fishes – and then another step down onto the beach of today.

It's the world, as William Blake didn't quite say, in a lump of sandstone.

In a story by Jorge Luis Borges, an old man sells him *The Book of Sand*, so called because you never see the same page twice, and neither the book nor the sand has any beginning or any end. The bookseller isn't named, but is from the Orkneys – an Old Red Sandstone man.

Millstone Grit

PEAK DISTRICT

Helen Mort

In the centre of my back, there's a large tattoo, the shape of a millstone. A border of leaves and ferns, black shading, intricate. Inside the frame, tiny trees, contour lines and numbers that mean Stanage Edge. A map of the landscape I think with. The place I'm standing shivering in now is somewhere in the right-hand corner of the map, somewhere towards the side of the tattoo. I place my left hand against rock. Autumn. Tuesday. The sky's the colour of an old trophy and the breeze is searching. The gritstone seems to keep the chill inside it the way a radiator keeps warmth. I brush my shoes against my trousers, lifting one foot first, then the other, wiping them carefully. I let my fingers move as they want. This is the ritual of climbing.

I hardly think about gritstone when I touch it now. It's so familiar. Coarse, angular grains under my palm. In places, climbers have worn the rock to a polish, a shiny, treacherous smoothness. The place where I want to put my foot at the moment is a gleaming scoop, impossible to stand on, 'Crack and Corner' corner. Severe. From a distance, this indent in the gritstone must look like a full stop. I need to step high, above the natural ledge.

Gritstone is a kind of sandstone. I remember learning about it in school before I ever understood what it was. Sedimentary rock, tight-packed grains. I used to say the word aloud: grit. It is utter hardness in the mouth, as if you're holding a tiny piece of grey rock on your tongue, running it over the roughness. Porous. Strongly cemented. Weak and strong layers. I knew the properties of gritstone before I understood what it was like to place my palms flat on a ledge of it and make a strange move called a 'mantleshelf', what it was like to reach high at the top of a route and grope for a hold, what it was like to trust in gritstone's friction on a cool day like this one.

The clouds shift and the whole landscape darkens. When I turn, there's a small bird of prey in the distance, circling. From the sky, Stanage must look like a strange wave. The UK is stippled with gritstone edges. Dividing lines. When I lived in Sheffield, this place always felt like a tide, the place where the city ran out and the Peak District began. Derbyshire is covered with gritstone escarpments, interrupting the moors and underlining the trees. In the east: Bamford, Stanage, Burbage, Frogatt, Baslow, Gardoms, Birchen, Harland. Out west: the Roaches, Hen Cloud, Ramshaw Rocks. But there is something tidal about Stanage. Around 300 million years ago in the Carboniferous period, a range of mountains were pushed up to the north and a river as big as something like the Mississippi spread its delta over much of what we now call England. As the delta built itself closer, sand and grit covered the shale and limestone layers. This kept shifting all the time – tides and strong currents moved and changed the sand banks and bars of the delta-forming layers (or deposits) that can be seen in an escarpment like Stanage. When I run along the top of the edge on a clear day, it does feel like following a river, pulled along by the current of the wind. As you walk towards the east end of Stanage, towards Apparent North and stare up, the lip of the rock seems to rear up. No wonder Ted Hughes likened this area to a huge wave about to crash down over Manchester.

I imagine the formation of gritstone like a climb in itself. The grit starting life on the floors or rivers and wide deltas. The climber gearing up on the ground, checking her harness, adding cams and nuts, quickdraw and slings, steady and slow, like the sediment, growing thicker. Then the pressure, the movement, the slow transformation. The climber's face, hard-set and focused with each move. And the uplift, the final exposure. A process that might have lasted minutes or forever.

The first route I ever climbed on gritstone was Flying Buttress (graded 'V Diff') with the poet Mark Goodwin. I hung on the rope and flailed around, seeing every tilt and difficulty as an overhang. It was a hot day and the gritstone seemed almost jewelled at the top in the sunlight. In his piece 'Museum of the Stanage-ophone', Mark describes the processes of compression and erosion that formed the edge, how, after the deposited particles of grit had been compacted and bonded hard:

> then patient weather set to work
> with its liquid chisel and file of air…

Mark's poem applauds the weird architecture of Stanage, the way it looks like something built: 'gothic / & modernist mixed, abrupt blocks / or intricate fins'. It notices the way in which slabs and buttresses seem 'decorated / with dark cracks & breaks' or 'frosted at their rims / with climbers' chalk'.

The title of Mark's poem, 'Museum of the Stanage-ophone' captures the eerie musicality of a gritstone edge like this. The liquid voice of a grouse. The chink of climbing gear, almost Alpine. But even as I start to climb now, in silence, route names crowd into my head. A mantra. A song. Anatomy. Andrea. Anniversary. Arete. Back to School. Badly Bitten. Butcher Crack. I love being here early, or late, or in bad weather. Times when everyone else has gone home. I imagine each empty route as a small stage. Cake stand. Carpe Diem. Cleft Wing Superdirect. Sometimes, I read the guidebook out loud as if I'm reading one of my poems, trying out lines. Dithering Frights. Divine Providence. Don't Fluff It. Fading Star. I try to match the diagrams and photographs to the looming shapes of the rock. Gargoyle Buttress. Gothic Armpit. Hold Your Breath and Hoaxer's Crack. In the evening, Stanage feels like a theatre with the curtain down, music-hall stage. Inverted V. Invisible Maniac. I imagine each route climbed for the first time. The held breath of the belayer. Kerb. King Kong and Kindergarten. Last Ice Cream. Louis the Loon. I think of Joe Brown and Alison Hargreaves, Ron Fawcett and Lucy Creamer. Imagine the act of naming a route for the very first time. Marmite. The Marmoset. Melancholy Witness. Namenlos. National Breakdown. Nihilistic Narl. I wonder what I'd call a gritstone route if I ever had the honour, repeat my favourite names again and again. Paradise Wall. Paradise Lost. Paralysis. Savage Amusement. Sithee Direct. I picture myself on routes I could never climb. The Unprintable. The Unthinkable. Wall of Sound. Then I turn back to the rock, my own hands and scuffed knuckles. My surprisingly still heart.

The guidebooks start with warnings:

> Climb the rock as it is. Do not be tempted to shape it to suit your inadequate skills or to gouge out protection placements where none exist.... Brushing with anything other than a toothbrush to remove excess chalk is rarely necessary. Once the hard exterior layer is removed, the softer sandy interior erodes very rapidly. If you cannot do a route or problem in its existing state, go away and train harder or accept that you aren't good enough...
>
> *Stanage Definitive*, 2001

I have only my body, inadequate, tentative, happy. I'm halfway up the corner now and the holds are better. Sometimes, when I'm climbing alone here and I look down, the millstones scattered below on the ground seem like strange eyes. Huge polo mints. Grey-green circles with holes in the middle. In the summer, they're hidden by bracken, but now they're bare and visible. If you've never seen a millstone before, you might come to Stanage and think they were alien deposits. And in a way, they are – relics from a lost age, abandoned, watching climbers swarm over the crag. It's reckoned there are probably 1,500 scattered throughout the Peak, but almost all of them are within a mile or so of a line drawn from Moscar to Fox House near Burbage and on to Dobb Edge.

Gritstone has been worked into tools to grind grain for thousands of years. You can see early evidence of this in querns – hand-powered stones, simple blunt cones and cylinders worked entirely by muscle which can still be found at Wharncliffe out near Stocksbridge, another place I like to climb in autumn, blocking out the hum of the bypass below. But the millstones that stand out are the ones once used in water, wind and steam mills. Circular millstones were once used in gristmills to grind wheat or barley. The mills would have a stationary stone or bedstone at the bottom and a turning runner stone above it which would spin to do the grinding. As I climb now, I think about that repetitive, endless act. I wonder if this landscape is a kind of bedstone, the climbers runner stones, circling up and down the rock, climbing and walking, always ending where we started. The first references to Peak District millstones are from the thirteenth century. They were quarried in the village of Hathersage – a place I used to live, staring at the hillside from my tiny cottage. Quarrying started in earnest in the fourteenth century and Derbyshire reached peak production in the sixteenth and seventeenth centuries. Along with lead mining, it became one of the area's main industries. The stones were sometimes called 'peaks'.

Traditionally, they were quarried by individual stonemasons, each making about sixteen pairs per year up on the hillside. A man and boy could produce a couple of stones in a month. They would then be transported down the hill and taken away by road or river, finding their way all over the UK. The labour of joining the stones with a wooden axle, hauling them up to the moorland and placing them in sledges is almost inconceivable. Climbing on the edge above them, I feel guilty for noticing each twinge in my forearms. Now, it's hard to image millstones at work, cast along the foot of the crag like beads fallen from a necklace, left where they were made. On my phone, I have a photo of my friend Jan at High Neb, standing and giving a thumbs up next to a millstone that someone has painted with a yellow curve and two dots, turning it into a beaming smiley face.

Peak District millstones were eventually phased out, overtaken by composite French stones, chert and cement. White bread had become fashionable and the French stones could produce white flour rather than the greyer substance from the Peak. As French stones became more and more popular, it is said that local workers attacked the mills in the Derwent Valley and destroyed stones. When I see them from above, there's something dark about the discs with their blank centres, as if the whole of this landscape's industrial past, slight now, invisible, could pass through the centre and dissolve. A vortex. The millstone is now the symbol of the Peak District National Park. It seems appropriate to Stanage, its complicated past and present, history as a loop, a circle, a lost stone with a hole in the middle, present and absent.

I'm about to top out, reaching over the lip of the rock and moving my feet up quickly. When I'm over, I turn and sit down on the edge, even though there's nobody to belay for, no rope to pull taut behind me. I look out towards the Hope Cement Works, strange and pale, remembering the elderly man, a dementia patient in a Bakewell hospital who once told me that Sheffield was always 'a dirty picture in a golden frame'. This view is the place where almost all my poems start, the place I imagine myself staring down from as I write. In 2012, I started work on a sequence addressed to the memory of Derbyshire climber Alison

Hargreaves, a world-class mountaineer who died descending from K2 in 1995. After her death, she was attacked in the media as a mother of two. Alison was the first woman to climb Everest unsupported, and soloed all the great north faces of the Alps in a single season. But when I try to imagine her, it's here, on gritstone, knuckles frayed and bleeding from hand jamming. Earlier this autumn, I came to Stanage Plantation to film a poem written as an address to her. The piece 'Dear Alison' imagines a route called Namenlos as a written place: 'late afternoon, and Stanage is a postcard to your loss, stamped with a daytime moon…. I write to you because your imprint's everywhere, across the landscape's leaned-on page.' Gritstone as parchment. A place I always go to find the right words.

Wherever I travel across the globe, I meet climbers who have been to Stanage and found it humbling. There is no point being half-hearted on gritstone. It's all or nothing. Exhilarating or brutally punishing. Peak limestone has delicacy, shine and curve. I've climbed on Welsh slate, on granite in Canada, on gneiss in East Greenland with majestic icebergs in the fjord below. But nothing is as satisfying as the feeling of your hands burning after a day on the grit, the bite of it, the sense of being still in the turning centre of a small, hard world.

Coal Measures

COALBROOKDALE

Paul Evans

There! Across the pool, behind the trees, surely a trick of the light – a movement. A woodcock rockets softly from a cleft in the bank above the swamp; two golden oak leaves drift down through trees. Rooks fall silent. Something opens, unfolding itself as if standing upright. There is a man in the woods. Chawtermaster Peake straightens himself, removes his bowler, takes out a handkerchief, blows his nose, wipes his eyes and whiskers. He has emerged from the darkness underground and, looking directly into the sun, he's blinded to me and the world as I see it. He opens his pocketwatch for the time: seven and twenty minutes past two o'clock in the afternoon of the winter of 1827. However unlikely it may be for us both to appear at the same time in the same place yet separated by 190 years, this apparition and I are bound by two things: blood and coal.

Here in the Short Woods, east of the Wrekin in Shropshire, a Chawtermaster (chartermaster) is like a tenant farmer, except that the land he rents is a hole in the ground. This hole is called Peake's Wood Pit and it leads below to where colliers pick at a black seam in a lightless tunnel, one of a dozen small mining ventures in these woods of the three hundred or more scratching at the edges of the Coalbrookdale coalfield. Peake has been to check on the workers he employs. I wonder how they're faring down there.

From the 1820s, the local press has been complaining of 'slavery' in these coal mines, children chained to tubs of coal and fed on gin and scalded bread to keep them keen. In 1842, the parliamentary Mines Report will shock the country with stories of children, five-year-olds working twelve-hour shifts for tuppence a day; girls and pregnant women whipped for slacking; boys and young men disfigured by the exertions of work and terrible injuries and deaths down there in the darkness. I want to believe Chawtermaster Peake is a fair man and not some monster presiding over subterranean atrocities, because I think his daughter or niece is my great-grandmother and so, however distantly, we are family. But I wonder if family respectability was bought with coal and I wonder if that carries a curse through the generations.

When I was a youth, I scrambled down an adit (the sloping tunnel of a drift mine) and had to wriggle under rocks of a roof collapse into an abandoned gallery. It felt like a crypt: its darkness tangible with the taste of rock dust bitter with memory – not just of those who worked and maybe died there but of the stone itself – a memory of the deep, deep past. It was not hard to imagine working a seam of coal two feet high and the ever-present risks of being crushed or succumbing to the damp. Blackdamp is carbon dioxide; undetectable, except that it chokes the songs out of canaries and drowns as surely as water. Firedamp is methane and can explode where it collects. Some time ago, firedamp ignited in an abandoned Short Woods pit and flames issued through holes in the ground as if from the gates of Hell. It burned on and off for years; 'damn kids' were blamed.

The years that separate me from Chawtermaster Peake are recorded in the tree rings of Short Woods oaks, now glowing like a cold furnace of winter sunlight. But the story of coal here is a more ancient one. In the nearby Roman city of Viraconium (now Wroxeter) the underfloor heating was produced by burning coal from this part of the Coalbrookdale coalfield where it outcrops or lies close to the surface. That was two thousand years ago, but before the Romans, people collected lumps of iron ore from the ground to smelt in charcoal-fired furnaces and manufactured the Iron Age. The first record for mineral extraction in this coalfield was in 1250, a right granted by Buildwas Abbey, not just for coal but also ironstone. In the Short Woods there's a spring oozing from a circle of birches where the ground is bare and the clay covered in rust: a bloody stain bearing testament to a coming revolution.

Lying beneath much of what is now Telford, the Coalbrookdale coalfield stretches nine miles from Linley near Broseley in the south-west to Lillishall in the north-east and is no more than three miles wide. It is described by the Shropshire Mining and Caving Club as 'a 20-metre-layer of Productive Coal Measures, on which Upper Coal Measures were deposited, in a series of folds, fractured by faults in a south-west-north-east orientation and divided by the Symon fault into an exposed western section [where the Short Woods are] – and a much deeper eastern section.'

The geological survey map for this area (SJ60) is a psychedelic swirl of colours representing one of the most complex geologies in the country. A muddy oak-gold colour shows the position of the rock under the Short Woods; the geological map describes it as 'middle coal measures of dominantly grey mudstones with many workable coals and ironstones, sandstones and fireclays.' Adjoining coalfield rock are later coal measures, 65 to 230 feet-thick of cream sandstones below, fireclays above and workable coals in the upper part in bedded mudstones. These coal measures were laid down in the tropical swamp forests of the Carboniferous period that began 354 million years ago and ended 64 million years later in catastrophic climate change. For 290 million years, the fossilised remains of the great forests of the Carboniferous lay dormant, sandwiched between the eroded dust of mountains, floating and folding in their journey over the surface of the Earth. Although the map appears to fix this seething chaos into permanence, I am reminded that cataclysmic events are not confined to aeons ago. It was a flood of Biblical proportions in the Pleistocene era, a mere blink of the geological eye, that allowed humans to get our mitts on coal and iron. Without that, we may not be standing now on the brink of another great change called the Anthropocene.

As the Ice Age began to thaw, about 15,000 years ago, melting glaciers from Wales and Northern England drained into a great lake geologists call Lake Lapworth that covered much of what is now north Shropshire and Cheshire. The River Severn originally flowed north from the glacial west. However, blocked from its northerly route to the sea at Chester, and pouring into the overflowing bathtub of Lake Lapworth, it eventually burst through the soft rocks at the northern end of Wenlock Edge, carving a ravine that drained the lake and sent the Severn southwards. This violent gouging of limestones, shales and coal measures of the Coalbrookdale coalfield created the Severn Gorge, exposing coal, iron ore, fireclay and limestone deposits, all of which – including the blood and bone of labour I am related to – became the raw materials for the Industrial Revolution.

The business of making iron in the Severn Gorge around Coalbrookdale had been fairly intense since medieval times when it was under monastic control. Through the abracadabra of geology that conjured all the necessary materials into one place, together with an insatiable human desire to control nature, this remote little valley became, quite literally, a crucible for industrial innovation and the modern world.

In 1709, the Coalbrookdale ironmaster Abraham Derby invented a way of smelting iron using coke instead of coal. Until then iron had been smelted in charcoal-powered furnaces, but the loss of British woodland had become dangerously unsustainable. Similar to the way in which wood is burned to produce charcoal, coal is burned to produce coke, a carbonised fuel that is lighter and can be heated to a much higher temperature. Derby was able to increase the size and productivity of blast furnaces making cast iron, and the Industrial Revolution exploded.

Coalbrookdale by Night was painted by Philip James de Loutherbourg in 1801, a century after Abraham Derby's coke innovation and when the Severn Gorge was aflame with furnaces and foundries. The scene is of furnaces near the Iron Bridge, open coke hearths of fire and smoke, cottages, a smithy, a joinery, an engine house, carthorses, a few ghostly people and strange iron forms like toppled monuments – it looks like ground zero of a disaster. This is a Romantic vision of Hell and yet there is a savage beauty to the fires of the aptly named Bedlam furnace flaring into the moonlit sky. I like to think the inferno is stoked by coke made from coal that was mauled out of a hole in the Short Woods by Peake, my collier ancestor. I like to think there is something heroic about this, but I fear it's a grim story of the exploitation of poverty for wealth and power, the hubris of Imperial ambition and, more lastingly, of the war against nature. I wonder what Chawtermaster Peake thought about the stuff he was hewing from the earth – what it was made of and how it got there – because I find it hard to get my head around coal.

I stand in the woods on such a winter's day and check my phone for the time: 14.27. Low sunlight slants through the grey trunks of alder trees to spotlight an emerald pool covered in duckweed and framed with sedges and horsetails. This stretch of swamp woodland along the lower edge of the Short Woods feels strange and foreboding; dead trees sinking into a bottomless black ooze seeping from the ground, a stink of decay. There is a mood here: a quiet, almost reverent melancholy, withdrawn from the world, something uncanny that I find eerily attractive. I pick a horsetail about 18 inches long from the mud; it's a jointed hollow stem ringed with whorls of simple filaments thin as daddy-longlegs. It may be a coarse, slight thing, a weedy green note in a greying world that breaks as I put it in my pocket, but the horsetail has a profound significance here. It is one of the few living survivors of the Carboniferous; it is the stuff that dreams, and coal, are made of.

Equisetum sylvaticum, the wood horsetail, snake grass or scouring rush is a 'living fossil' in that it belongs to a group of plants recorded from fossils that once grew in the coal forests of the Carboniferous. Imagine 300 million years ago, plants like this grew 100 feet tall and were still dwarfed by tree ferns and club mosses towering above them. The coal forests grew on flat land flooded by rivers, like the Amazon rainforest today, but their environment and inhabitants were very different. Many of the old pictorial representations of the coal forest borrow from the 'dismal swamp' idea of interpreters, who compared it to the wet woodlands of their own experience but with an absence of seasonal flowers, a dominance of 'primitive' plants, populated by slithering, cold-blooded things and creepy crawlies. Although there were no flowering plants and the amphibians such as crocodiles had yet to evolve into reptiles, mammals and birds, the dominant animals were gloriously diverse, dizzyingly brilliant and huge insects.

Coal forests were massive, global ecosystems and responsible for pumping oxygen levels in the atmosphere up to 35 percent, the highest in geological history. Today, oxygen is just 21 percent. Insects are restricted in size by the amount of oxygen they can breathe through holes in their exoskeletons, and so, although a dragonfly emerging from this pool in the Short Woods is identical to one 300 million years ago, the Meganeura, giant dragonflies of the coal forest with a wingspan of 25 inches, are extinct. These vast levels of oxygen are one half of the coal forest equation; the other is the carbon laid down in the peat formed by decaying vegetation. In the endless green tropical summer of the Carboniferous, the photosynthesis of the coal forest split carbon dioxide into its component parts: oxygen and carbon. The oxygen was released into the atmosphere and the carbon locked in the peat.

'Coal' is the silent forest, the answer to the question: 'If a tree falls in a forest and there is no one to hear it, does it make a sound?' first asked by philosopher George Berkeley in 1710, a year after Abraham Derby's coke-instead-of-coal invention. Coal is an answer to the possibility of unperceived existence. How can we perceive this challenge from the Enlightenment? How do we respond to the life of a forest that existed before we even evolved? We set fire to it, that's what we do.

What dies in the coal forest falls into the water: horsetails, tree ferns, dragonflies and crocodiles rot under the surface of the swamp where a lack of oxygen creates layers of peat. The biological decomposition by microbes is a process that turns what is largely wood, resistant to decay because of its lignin content, into organic carbon. Tightly packed in layers, the peat becomes part of the geological process and compressed and heated into coal; different carbon concentrations make different kinds of coal – anthracite, bituminous and lignite. Although geological processes have distributed coal measures around the world, they are finite and do not occur much later than the Carboniferous period. Recent research finds that a fungus – an Agariomycete like fly agaric – evolved at the end of the Carboniferous with an enzyme capable of degrading lignin. This may be a clue as to why there's an end to coal.

In later periods, dead forests produced carbon dioxide instead of coal. Towards the end of the Carboniferous there was a period of climate change. The effect on the coal forest ecosystems was cataclysmic. Many species became extinct. Whole forests vanished. Does this sound horribly familiar? Ashes to ashes, dust to dust, geologically speaking.

Peake's Wood Pit is lost from the map. Many of the big pits in the Coalbrookdale coalfield were nationalised and we know what happened to the coal industry; none survives. The last Short Woods mine closed in 1970, but, despite fierce local opposition, much of the surrounding land was opencast to scrape up the last remnants of coal. To me, this had the feeling of a lobotomy, as if the memory of the land itself had been surgically removed. Many suspect that, like other opencast sites, it will be developed for housing. Telford prides itself on being the Birthplace of Industry, which is not really true, but not the Birthplace of Global Warming, which is not really fair.

As I stand in the wood there is movement through the trees: a group of fallow deer, their backs black as coal, disappear like ghosts into the dusk. I hear the clash of antlers as bucks fight beneath oaks on the old mine workings; badgers wake in their sunken yards; woodcock turn their oilcan faces to the ferns. Chawtermaster Peake replaces his bowler, turns towards the dark cleft and before the two oak leaves that the bird dislodged touch the ground, he steps into shadow and is swallowed up.

Shale

THE WEALD

Neil Ansell

I am walking on sunshine. The path that I am following leads through a coppice thick with bluebells. A buzzard circles high above the trees. Robins and wrens dash from bush to bush, staying low. Pheasants clatter away in every direction. And then there is a sudden burst of song, a song so powerful, so incandescent, that it sweeps through the wood like wildfire. A nightingale; not something that you hear too often these days, but this is their sole remaining heartland, their last redoubt. This is the Weald, sandwiched between the North and South Downs and spanning four counties. From the summit of the Downs it looks idyllic, a great bowl thick with trees and the occasional church spire from one of the thinly scattered villages.

The word 'weald' is from the Old English for 'forest', and this was once the home of a great wildwood. The soil here – sands, clays, sandstone and shale – is good for trees, not so good for agriculture. Even now it is the most densely wooded part of England. It is an ancient land, too, in geological terms an anticline, or an inversion, eroded down to deeper, older soils. In the early 1800s, a local doctor and amateur geologist, Gideon Mantell, or according to some stories his wife Mary, found some fossilised teeth not far from here. He recognised them as resembling the teeth of an iguana, only twenty times larger, and named the animal from which they came an iguanadon, the very first dinosaur to be identified as such. These are Jurassic soils.

Two hundred million years ago the sun beat down on a shallow sea, and its energy was captured by planktonic algae, the base of a prehistoric food chain. When these cells died, as all life must, they sifted down to the sea bed in a seemingly endless rain of organic matter and mixed with clay, silt and mud. As the layers were buried deeper and deeper, these sediments began to change under the influence of heat and pressure and time – millions and millions of years of it – until they became beds of shale, thick with oil. So when I say I am walking on sunshine, it is true; deep beneath my feet is fossilised sunshine.

Back on the roadside, the verges are overgrown with pale-mauve cuckoo flowers, above which flitter orange-tip butterflies, and the fence behind them bears signs warning of high-tech security monitoring, of covert devices, of thermal imaging cameras and forensic marking. And now a sign warning that guard dogs are on patrol. And legal warnings that there is at all times someone on site opposed to entry, and that any attempt to force entry could result in imprisonment. In a woodland clearing outside a small English village in deepest Sussex is not necessarily the first place you would expect to find an oil well, but there it is; a slab of concrete not much bigger than a tennis court, encircled by an impressive array of razor wire.

There is one more sign: an expired notice of a planning application for major development – flow testing of the existing hydrocarbon lateral borehole, together with a testing flare and a security upgrade. This application is a done deal now; while the local parish council voted unanimously against it, the final say went to the county council, which voted unanimously in favour.

This is Balcombe in West Sussex, pretty much the ground zero of British anti-fracking protests. Now at the time of writing there are more than 250 local anti-fracking groups in the UK, with more being formed all the time, but five years ago this was largely new territory. This quiet country road was blockaded by hundreds of protestors, and there were mass arrests. The following year the company concerned suspended operations at this particular hydrocarbon site, but it was not a matter of public relations; rather it was in response to a global fall in oil prices which rendered this kind of energy-intensive extraction less financially viable. The answer to virtually any question as to why the world is the way that it is is almost always: the economy.

Licences for oil and gas exploration have been granted across great blocks of our countryside; a million acres of our country have been put up for grabs. These southern shale beds are thought to contain oil, while further north the shale fields would need to be fracked for gas. Licences have been permitted across a continuous band of northern England from coast to coast, through Lancashire and Yorkshire and down into the East Midlands. There could be drilling beneath our national parks, beneath residential areas. The oil companies assert that the environmental damage would be minimal, and it is true that a small site such as at Balcombe might have only a small footprint, compared to say opencast mining, but the fact remains that to extract all the available resources there would need to be many thousands of such sites, packed together in clusters across the vast oil and gas fields. Not much actual fracking has taken place so far; what we are seeing is a handful of exploratory sites and a granting of permissions, laying the groundwork for a great oil rush the moment the economy demands it.

This is not a conversation that I envisaged we would be having; I had assumed that we were past this. I thought that we were talking about developing renewable energy as quickly as possible, to a point where we could start to leave existing fossil fuels in the ground, for the sake of the environment, rather than scrabbling about looking to squeeze every last drop out of more and more marginal sites. But it is not in the nature of business to turn down an opportunity for money to be made, and it is not in the nature of many of us to pass on the convenience afforded us by an energy-intensive lifestyle.

Oil shale is the source of almost all fossil fuels, save for coal. It is hard to overstate the impact it has had on our lives, for good and ill; not only is it the source material of almost all our energy consumption, it is also the original ingredient of all our plastic production. I like to imagine that the plastic of the computer on which I type could be built from the bones of my ancestors. Shale is the bedrock of human progress, and likely also the bedrock of our own destruction. The traditional oil well or gas rig is where the oil and the natural gas have been squeezed out of the rock and into underground reservoirs. Fracking is a means of extracting these resources from the rock itself, by hydraulic fracturing. For oil shale to 'mature' it needs to have been subjected to huge temperatures and pressures, so most of it occurs in bands of sediment that are now perhaps a mile underground. The reason the oil shales of the Weald are so particularly tempting to developers is because more recent soils have been weathered away. Here the oil-shale bands are embedded in the Kimmeridge Clay just half a mile deep. Half the depth means less cost of extraction. Economics.

Half a mile may seem close to an oil company, but it is too much for me. For a rock that is found over such huge swathes of the world, beneath land and sea, shale remains out of sight. It does not make mountains. If I am to hold it in my hands, I need to go elsewhere.

Kimmeridge Bay, on the Jurassic coast of Dorset, is not the easiest place to get to, not for someone without a car. When I was an idealistic teenager, way back in the late seventies, it seemed to me that there were already too many cars using too much fuel, driving on too many roads and causing too much pollution. It felt self-evident that there needed to be a vanguard of people who said no to cars, and if not me then who? Forty years on, and I am still waiting for much of a groundswell of people who have come to the same conclusion.

Kimmeridge is a tiny, pretty thatched village on Dorset's Isle of Purbeck. As I drop down towards the village, a pair of kestrels and a pair of buzzards are hovering at the ridgeline, poised in the updraught, and the red flags are raised to warn that the neighbouring military firing range is in use. The village is isolated; it has no shops and no bus service, but what it does have is a fossil museum and an oil well, and a rock form named after it. I have timed my visit well; for the past two days there has been heavy rain, but today is glorious spring sunshine. From the village it is a further half mile or so down to the shore. I walk down the slipway to the bay, and past the skull of a stranded fin whale, which has an explanatory sign beside it. There are few people here in spite of the fine weather, just a handful of dog walkers and a couple of surfers out on the water, waiting to catch a wave.

Tall, crumbling cliffs of Kimmeridge Clay stretch out along the coast in either direction, and there is a sign warning of recent rock falls. The beach below the cliffs is a flat stone platform littered with fallen boulders. In places this stone platform stretches out into the sea in jetties, cracked into blocks that fit perfectly together like an Inca wall. The cliff face is banded with strata: thick layers of oil shale laid down millions of years apart, and thinner bands of white limestone and basalt. The exposed layers of shale in these cliffs do not so much emerge from the land into the sea, as from the sea into the land – there is a huge bed of shale here beneath the English Channel, which just barely touches the land at a short stretch of this coastline.

The fallen shale has weathered to a dark grey, but where it is freshly shattered it is as black as oil, and almost sticky, bituminous. I pick up a small fragment and touch it with the flame from a cigarette lighter. It scorches, and a pungent smelling smoke curls out of it. Some of these beds of shale contain as much as seventy percent hydrocarbons.

As I follow the coast I begin to notice the fossils embedded in the stone at my feet, vast numbers of tiny massed shells and the occasional ammonite. Some of these are just an inch or two across, while some stretch to almost a foot in diameter. A huge array of fossilised fish has been found here on this coastline, as well as ichthyosaurs and plesiosaurs and crocodilians, and much more. A whole long-gone ecosystem preserved in stone. It makes the past feel very close. I am distracted by a cormorant doing a fly-by, low and near, and then I hear a quiet, rising trickle, as of water. It is a rain of fine stone, pouring down the face of the cliff above me and piling into a mound at the foot of the cliff. That warning sign was not kidding. Erosion in action. It is not often we get to see geological action on a human timescale.

I retrace my steps back to the bay and climb to the clifftop path. Just to the west of the little beach is the oil pump, and I want to take a look while I am here. It is a beam pump or pumpjack, also known as a nodding donkey, and it has been extracting oil here non-stop, rising and falling steadily like a perpetual motion machine, since before I was born. It is said to be the oldest continuously operating oil pump in Britain. It seems strangely out of place here in the bucolic English countryside, right by the seashore. The last time I saw one of these was when I was hitching America coast to coast, and crossed the oilfields of the Texas panhandle. There was an entire landscape of them, a forest of them, from horizon to horizon. My rejection of the car did not quite extend to a reluctance to take up an empty seat in a vehicle that was already on the road.

As I stand on the clifftop, peering through the chainlink fence, gazing at the strangely graceful and balletic motion of the pump, I am joined by a dog-walker with a cocker spaniel. He comes here often, he tells me, it is a favourite spot. On the cliff face immediately below us, he says, you can see the oil seeping from between the rocks, and they are sticky to the touch. It is beautiful, he says, and I suppose that it is, inexplicably, though I consider to myself that an asteroid about to strike the earth would likely be a thing of terrible beauty, too.

The swallows are skimming the sunlit fields where the year's newborn lambs are playing, there is the repeated whomp of artillery from the neighbouring firing range that echoes off the cliffs, and the pump just keeps on pumping, rising and falling, like a bell tolling.

Hydrocarbons

NORTH SEA

Esther Woolfson

Abright midwinter afternoon and I've come back here to walk, to a place I know well, to this long, empty beach; behind me, high wind-formed dunes, in front of me, the North Sea, today a benign prospect of even, silvered calm. On the horizon, the usual line of huge, grey vessels heads towards oil rigs far out at sea. Today though, they seem becalmed, like a fleet of shadows. Perhaps it's just the way the light's falling, or a matter of perception that they seem immobile. Once, in the days when the oil business was booming, there was an air of urgency about the continuous plying to and fro of these vessels supplying and supporting the life and work of the offshore oil industry, a sense of bustling progress, but now, everything has changed.

As I walk here beside the low, clear waves, I know I'm looking for the invisible, seeking to explain things which, in the usual run of things, we hardly know are there. They must exist because everything around us tells us that they do, more so possibly than any other substances on Earth. There's nothing more important, more potent – all the more so, paradoxically, in their diminishing. Oil, petrol, gas; these hydrocarbons which, by our burning of them, are destroying the world.

Although similarly products of Time itself, hydrocarbons are different from the components of Earth's lithic history, from the solidity of stone and rock. For most of us, they're never seen, as if there's nothing there. There's little to touch, nothing to crunch underfoot, to run through our fingers, to collect up, to turn into mementoes as we do pebbles from beach or mountain. Although we're surrounded by their products and influences, the only time most of us see them is in the quick gush of clear liquid as we fill the tanks of our ever-thirsty cars. They're there, too, in the faint, lingering smell of petrol as we do, the warm gust of aviation fuel as we cross a runway, the whisper and flare of the gas turned on. Even though almost unseen, we know that in every way, these substances have driven our contemporary world.

On these days of low winter sun, the city, a few miles south, seems melted into a haze of gilded light. Aberdeen – 'the oil capital' – is transformed from its usual aspect of unforgiving greys to one of misty gold. This once quiet city, a place of solid Victorian grandeur hewn from glittering grey stone, its economic roots founded in fishing, granite quarrying and farming, its cultural ones in its ancient, distinguished academic record of ecclesiastics, philosophy and natural history, has been changed by hydrocarbons. In such a short time, the confident permanence of granite has been shaken by the fleeting evanescence of oil and gas.

Although exploration had taken place for a long time beforehand, in 1969 huge deposits of oil were found in the North Sea between Norway and Scotland. The geological processes of 'rifting', the pulling apart of the tectonic plates of Earth's lithosphere during the Triassic and Jurassic periods, created most of the conditions which would allow the development of hydrocarbons during the Late Jurassic and Early Cretaceous periods, between 150 and 66 million years ago.

Hydrocarbons – organic chemical compounds composed only of the elements carbon and hydrogen – are the main constituents of petroleum and natural gas which, together with coal, make up the three primary fossil fuels, those atmosphere-destroying remnants of plant and animal life long-ago. Liquid hydrocarbons are formed by organic matter, heat and time with the decomposition of aquatic organisms, prehistoric zooplanktons and algae remaining in conditions of low oxygen for hundreds of millions of years. Through chemical processes and compaction, they break down to form kerogen and bitumen which change in a process called catagenesis, as heat and pressure degrade the kerogen to form hydrocarbon chains. The prevailing conditions determine the nature of the hydrocarbons. The formation of petroleum reserves requires a very particular range of temperatures: the 'petroleum window', between 50° and 150°C, is required to form oil; and the 'gas window' between 150° and 200°C for gas. The accumulations form in 'source rock' which, in the North Sea, is most often in a substance called Kimmeridge Clay, from where they migrate and collect in reservoirs of porous rock to be sealed in 'traps' by shale, mudstone or salt.

The quantities are difficult to imagine. One industry source suggests that production from one field found in 1998 could fuel a family car for almost 1,700 years, or heat water for 4.5 million showers.

These almost-mystic products of the Earth have flared and burned throughout history and although many of us believe their use to be a recent development, it isn't. In China, that oracular philosophical text, the I Ching, compiled around 800 BC, describes natural gas burning: 'above fire, below, the lake', while techniques for oil drilling were well developed by the Warring States period, around 400 BC. Herodotus, Plutarch and Marco Polo all commented on their observations of the use or presence of oil. There were and are places in ancient Mesopotamia, now Iraq, and in Azerbaijan, where oil drips, seeps and floats to leave its inimitable polychromic patterns on water, where it bubbles from the surface of the Earth, but although used for heat and light and even medicinally for thousands of years, it wasn't until the growth of industry in America and Europe in the mid-nineteenth century, that its large-scale exploitation began. The combined efforts of the triumvirate of Nikolaus Otto, inventor in 1876 of the four-stroke engine, Karl Benz who developed Otto's ideas to manufacture his first four-wheeled car in 1893, and Henry Ford, the first to use assembly lines for industrial production, brought about the vast expansion of this new age of 'power'.

'Power' – a word to remind us that oil is more than it is, than it seems to be. How did the ancient remains of early life become 'power'? We might have thought once that hydrocarbons were life itself, but didn't know that they contained their own end, too; that in this, the substance of the history of Earth, was to be the measure of ourselves. No longer revering them as a mystery, with their alchemy of heat and light, we began to look on them as a gift of gold. Cause and motive, they have been the foundation of acts of political infamy – the overthrow in 1953 by Britain and America of the elected leader of Iran, Mohammad Mosaddeq, whose attempt to regain control of his country's oil reserves was seen as a threat to Western interests, the more recent wars waged for the strategic and economic interests of the West, and now, the continuing conflicts between concern and greed, reality and denial.

I look out past the clear rills of water at my feet towards the places where those subterranean landscapes lie, inverse worlds of deep clefts and valleys, sandstone and shale, almost emptied now of their fiery secrets. They are worlds of yin and yang, cool and heat, concealed and obvious. The invisible and the volatile are set against the solid vastness of the structures created to find and drill and store and sell.

The headquarters and offices, the vessels and pipelines, which came into being after the discovery of oil here, are all super-scale, huge, male, 'yang'. It has always been a man's industry, a macho one. Of course, many women work in it, too, but the image, and actuality, have been of unyielding exclusivity and swagger, all Red Adair and poster photos of hard men in hard hats and many kinds of danger.

Here, in Aberdeen's parks there are monuments to its victims: the memorial in Hazlehead Park to the 167 men lost in the *Piper Alpha* oil rig explosion of 1988, the worst ever in a hazardous industry. In Johnson Gardens, above the Japanese terraces, the pond and blue-painted bridge, is a granite cairn engraved with the names of the sixteen people killed in a helicopter crash in 2009, only one of many in which oil workers have been sacrificed to the world's desires. As I walked there recently on a dark and rainy afternoon, the song playing in my head was Leonard Cohen's cool adaptation of the beautiful, terrifying thousand-year-old Jewish liturgical poem, the *Unetanneh Tokef*. Its words: 'And who by water, and who by fire' might have been written for oil workers injured or killed, not just by water or fire but by chain, too, by crane, by rope, by explosion, not only here but everywhere oil is delved from earth and sea.

Hydrocarbons brought outsiders to this once inward-looking city. For years, many houses in my street were occupied by Americans. My daughters played with neighbours' children in the Saturday baseball league in the playing fields above the city. In teams sponsored by oil companies, they became 'Oil-tool Braves' and 'Wireline Dodgers,' surrounded by the coolboxes and high-octane enthusiasm with which American parents participated in those communal events, but now, so many years on, their baseball bats and caps lie, as these things do, in the small domestic museum of the accumulated past. My neighbours, as most of the American community, are gone. They were always transients, passing clouds which leave nothing behind, a presence too light for roots.

Over the years, I learned most about oil from walking through the streets near my home, past large Victorian houses turned in the 1970s and 1980s into offices to meet the demands of oil and gas. I learned from signs on gates, from names and words: subsea, platform, drilling, pumping, exploration, cables, fluids, hydraulics, pipelines, wellhead, diving, valves, explosives, seismic, safety, risk, emergency. Often, company names were engraved on slabs of granite and marble and sometimes, a logo would conjure the immaterial in the familiar language of business: *premier*, *solutions*, *competency*, *evolution*. The gods were here too: Triton and Neptune, Apollo, Poseidon, Oceanus, supreme in their command of these deep and dangerous seas – but now, the gods have fled.

In 2009, the oil price was $150 a barrel. Today, it's nearer a third of that. In 2014, 450,000 people worked in the UK oil industry; last year, it was 330,000. Unit operating costs fell by half in the past two years and industry expenditure fell from £26 billion to £17.2 billion in the same time. There's no definitive way of knowing how much oil we've used or how much is left.

Once, you could walk the quays of Aberdeen Harbour, gaze up at huge vessels preparing to sail and listen to voices shouting, to gain the sense of this unknown life of oil, but now, the whole harbour's surrounded by chain-link fences, intercoms, gates and guards. The supply ships that snout against the quayside walls still give the air of being about to break through to advance hungrily on the adjacent Georgian streets, warehouses and sailors' rests.

The city fades into afternoon light. A few smaller vessels nearer to shore float like toys, blue and red on luminescent water. It's late now for birds, only a few gulls overhead and the brisk flight of roosting jackdaws across the dunes. Once, people gave oilfields the names of birds: Shearwater, Fulmar, Buzzard, Gannet, Golden Eagle, Merganser, Kittiwake, Heron, Cormorant.

An estimated million birds died after the *Deepwater Horizon* disaster in Louisiana in 2013, 225,000 after the *Exxon Valdez* disaster in 1989, a further half million or so killed every year by oil spills. Marine mammals, sea turtles, fish, crustacea, too, the life of earth and sea being destroyed twice over, by oil and by its planetary effects.

The first warning we had of them was in 1895 when the Swedish physical chemist Svante Arrhenius presented a paper on the effects that burning hydrocarbons would have on Earth's atmosphere, but when, over the years, voices continued to warn, we weren't listening.

Now, here, everything is different, although it hasn't been the prospect of devastating climate change that has brought about alteration in this city's fortunes but the vagaries of markets, the world's cruel, illogical imperatives. The symbols of power are still here, but their potency has gone. The air is still loud with the unquiet engines of the favoured vehicles of the city's once-oil-rich, but they seem to roar on in growing silence. Houses, offices, company headquarters are empty. Where signs have gone, revenant images linger on stone or wood, in blank spaces where nameplates once were. Stoic talk of 'optimism' is belied by the unspoken reproaches of carved granite and engraved brass. The new words are 'decommissioning, well-plugging, abandonment'. The cost of 'decommissioning' – the removal of massive oil platforms – is expected to be £2 billion this year alone. Aberdeen University now offers a degree course in Decommissioning.

The sky glows in a last, late flare as darkness approaches over what, in the oil industry, is called 'the United Kingdom Continental Shelf', down from the Arctic and Norway, over Faroe and Shetland, over the many installations far out at sea, over oilfields both working and abandoned, over lit and busy platforms and those now redundant, waiting to be broken up.

Here, we seem caught between endings, the fate of the city or the Earth. I think of the hundreds of millions of years that went into making these finite substances and the brief flash of time in which we have almost used them up. I walk back across the darkening beach, the city lighting up in front of me. The sea seems reassuring, enduring as the visible and invisible merge in darkness. I wonder what could have been different, what we might have known or done or changed. On the horizon, the ships' lights, too, are coming on in the dark, like a string of fairylights decorating the edge of earth and almost empty sea.

Limestone Secrets

DERBYSHIRE

Sue Clifford

I grew up in the Carboniferous. We burned geological specimens on our fire, we breathed gases transformed and captured over 300 million years ago in great swamps and estuaries, which still have me wheezing. We sometimes found shiny bits of tree and fern prints in the coal bucket, and we knew enough to ask – were they from High Main, Top Hard, Waterloo seams? Around us in valleys made by nature, winding gear trundled daylong, nightlong and pit tips grew from black fins to whalebacks to unnatural grazed hills.

People somehow imagine that town and country are separate entities, contrasting realities. But my experience was of town and village, heavy industry, mine, mill and factory, jostling with farm and forest. Robin Hood was a local hero, D. H. Lawrence walked down our road. Easy to see how my abiding interest has been in how things collide, accumulate, overlay or get scoured away. Fascination with the land and with nature can only have been helped by walking, cycling, riding in ever-increasing circles.

From the brow of the hill I could see a lighthouse. Its beam languidly punctuated the night sky, which was hardly dark, given the twenty-four-hour working pit in the valley foreground. The ray sped the ten crow-miles from this limestone inlier of Derbyshire to the home Coal Measures of Nottinghamshire. Crich Stand, the lighthouse, is about as far from the sea as you can be in England. A tower of wood had been built here in the 1760s on an old beacon site, simply to enjoy the long, long views. Other towers followed, the latest in memory of the fallen in the Great War, rebuilt as the quarry edge receded.

For me the beam prompted reveries of valleys, edges, sky, distance, stars, the hugeness of everything; the smallness of me, of us. When I studied geography later, the vast timeframe, wandering continents and myriad creatures turned to stone stacked into the stratigraphical column never struck me with such exotic force as that siren call.

During the Carboniferous period, extensive seas gave way to estuaries and forests, leaving us limestones, sandstones and coal, and when I was small we had the run of them.

We travelled a lot in the limestone of the White Peak in particular, the pale stone distinguishing it from the nearer millstone grit of the Dark Peak. Staying in a farmhouse in the dales where Derbyshire and Staffordshire meet, we lingered around the white stone farm, opening the gate to let occasional cars through, a penny for our work. The valley behind had no stream but it had rock faces, some nursery crags to climb, with ferns tucked into every hand- and foothold, and there were pale-yellow rock roses and delicate sky-blue harebells. The earth seemed light, bright, somehow shining back, rather than absorbing, the sun. Downhill, I spent hours uncovering shy bullheads under the stones of a tiny stream that chuckled into the River Manifold.

'Manyfold' is the domestic name – it means the same as Meander, the river in Turkey that gave us the word and which nonchalantly ambles across its flat floodplain to the Mediterranean. But this small stream's many folds wriggle between vertical cliffs. I have an eighteenth-century etching of it, called *A Prospect on the River Manyfold at Wetton Mill*, dated July 29, 1743, by Thomas Smith of Derby. In the foreground, men point at the marvel of the pale, slabbed crags.

Further down the valley, the River Manifold sometimes performs magic. In drought, the water simply slips away between the stones. And revealed is a secret world. I would be enraptured, in the dry riverbed among the tumble of rocks where brown trout and bullhead should swim and armoured caddisfly larvae should creep.

One story of limestone is the story of water, gravity, secrets and dyes. Dyes poured down the sinkholes revealed the waters' reappearance into its surface course three miles along. Near Ilam are the Boiling Holes graphically describing the scene where the Manifold finds the light again after journeying through caves of its own making. It is an unsteadying experience, seeing turmoil in a riverbed, even when you know the reason.

All over limestone country water dramatically or stealthily makes its way down, at the insistence of gravity. In some places its work has achieved grand, dripping caverns. At the same time, slow drippings of calcium-laden water precipitate the lime to create stalactites of great stature and complexity dangling from cave roofs, their dripped-on partners below, the stalagmites, attempting gravity-defying structures. Cavers have provided evocative names, in the Peak Cavern for example: Lumbago Walk, Beer Monsters Secret Tap Room, Orchestra Passage, Pluto's Dining Room, the Devil's Staircase, Perseverance Pot.

Also above Castleton in Derbyshire, the most enchanting cavern for us as children was the Speedwell Mine, for here you have to clamber into a boat and be rowed gently through the man-made tunnels that link mining adits with natural caverns now inhabited by water. This elfin-led journey linked the power of human endeavour and the force of the natural – the complications of underground.

And there is always the moment when the guide tells you he is about to turn off all the lights. A click and you are not in shade, not gloom, not twilight – but blackness. It is nothing like simply closing your eyes in the dark, for this darkness is so profound that your very heart tunes to the earth.

Not only black but quiet, save for somewhere a drip, a constant time-keeper, a reminder that you are connected somehow to the beyond, the above, the below – that gravity and time hold you, despite all your senses floating free. It is hard to know where you begin and end, if you even exist.

There is terror here, too – the easily roused fear of things that you cannot see, fear of incarceration with your imagination and that of your forebears. The boat, the rowing, the River Styx, the Lethe, a jumble of Hades and Pluto, of dragons and boggarts – not the realm of fire, not the inferno, but water and dark and petrification – the Underworld.

Across the White Peak, villages and towns still thank the gods for a sustained water flow; they wouldn't be there without it. In the summer months, well-dressings celebrate the permanent springs and even old taps. Boards, clay-covered, with flowers and berries pressed into the soft, damp substrate, show biblical scenes, or revel in the richness of the local flora, fields and drystone walls.

Peter's Stone is a coral-reef knoll as big as a church between Wardlow and Litton in Derbyshire, framed in a streamless, cliffed valley. Three hundred and fifty million years ago, fish grazed this coral reef in a warm Carboniferous sea. Other layered limestones have the gentlest of origins in shallowish, quiet, warm seas. Away from the violating influence of mud and sand, marine creatures of many kinds, having taken up calcium dissolved in seawater to protect or rigidify themselves, die, and softly settling, compressed by the weight of subsequent layers, the bodies and precipitates harden into stone.

Wherever you step into the carbon cycle, the process sounds simple. Rain, as it falls, gathers carbon dioxide (or sulphur dioxide or nitrous oxide from burning coal and oil), becomes more acid. Carbonic acid will dissolve, just a little, any lime-rich surface that it lands upon and wanders across. However hard and massive, mountain limestone is permeable. Faults and joints give ways in, uneven surfaces gather puddles and pools buying time for water to etch and eat ways down. As Norman Nicholson puts it in his poem 'Beck':

> The falling water
> hangs steady as stone;
> But the solid rock
> Is a whirlpool of commotion.

Wildness is the hallmark of mountain limestone landscapes. Ice played its part scouring the rock, frost fracturing the surfaces, and then melting and gushing. In Yorkshire, this gives us clints and grykes (limestone pavement), swallets and sinkholes, dry waterfalls, reef knolls, gorges, crags, scars, caves. This is real karst topography.

A world map of karst takes us from the source of early excitement and naming on the Italian–Slovenian border (the word 'karst' meaning 'rocky, barren land'); to the Burren, in the west of Ireland, with its exquisite flora hiding in the cracks of limestone pavement; Viñales in western Cuba, where salt pots and jellymoulds abruptly rise from a plain; Yunnan and those scenes from Chinese paintings – vast colonies of uncanny pinnacles; the tropics' vast underground caverns, where fresh and salt water mix; rainforest caves hung with bats and heaped with guano; and the caves of the Dordogne, with their enigmatic signs of human culture, echoes of the word 'karst' appearing in the place names 'Carcassonne' and the 'Causses'.

In Yorkshire, cavers drop 360 feet alongside a waterfall into Gaping Ghyll. Boggart's Roaring Holes, Hell Hole, Jingling Pot and Rumbling Hole send more than a frisson as I remember the breaths of wind, the water's rush, the dark.

On the tops, hart's-tongue fern loves the lime and the damp, it seeks shelter in the clefts in the limestone pavement and decorates the rims of pots. In areas where lime is scarce, archaeologists might use this fern as an indicator of building, its predilections giving away traces of lime mortar, very useful for the forensic tracking of lost mills.

Walking across the limestone of the Carboniferous one must be wary – not only of the clints, sinks and swallets, but also of shafts and poisoned heaps of spoil. Memories of digging are everywhere, not just huge and domestic quarries for building and roadstone, lime and cement, but domestic delving for minerals cooled from volcanic and plutonic activities along fault lines sometimes miles long. In Derbyshire, swarms of hillocks, waste from workings along mineral veins betray lines of rakes, scrins, flats and pipes, rich in galena, leading you on to old smelting sites. Some workings stretch back for two millennia; Youlgreave means 'old workings', so, already antique when the Saxons named it. Pigs of lead from Roman exploitation are found here and there.

Lime-loving spring sandwort is a giveaway – it's known as leadwort here, and alpine pennycress attempts to colonise bare heaps. The miners were farmers, too, and knew well the lethal nature of lead. They planted ash trees and sycamores along old rake lines to keep the grass down in an attempt to safeguard the animals. Farming and industry struggled side by side or one atop the other; six hours below hacking and hauling, six working the land on top, except when the season or weather suggested a break in pattern.

Carboniferous limestone country has given us lime for the fields, copper, lead, zinc, silver. What was once waste is now prized; fluorspar is the basis of fluorine used in medicine, enamelling and as a flux in iron-making. You might find barytes in your toothpaste, calcite-rich paint picking out the middle of the road, underlain by lime roadstone, edged by concrete kerbstones, lined with limestone buildings held together by lime mortar or cement.

November – in the Jurassic, standing at Portland Bill on my own in the dark with the lighthouse beam inhibited by a miasma which prompted the moan of the great foghorn – I am transported back to the silent landlocked beacon of my childhood. Birdwatchers say that on clear nights in spring this beam picks out migrant birds in the dark.

When I first spent time on the Isle of Portland in Dorset, it was with a wonderfully mixed group of students of architecture, planning, building and geology. I led them on an exploration of one of the great building stones that gave face to their alma mater, University College London. UCL, 'the godless college of Gower Street', is graced with a Neoclassical portico and front quadrangle fashioned in the 1820s from Portland stone. It had never been finished and as a 150th-anniversary project, money was raised to complete some of the buildings. By 1983, work was beginning and I had shaped a project to help students to link design and building with the impact of their decisions.

They knew Portland stone in passing from their college buildings and from London's streets, perhaps even from buildings in India, Hong Kong and New Zealand.

Hardly anchored by over twenty miles of Chesil Beach, the Isle of Portland projects into the Channel with cliffs made vertical by hard stone worked by an aggressive sea. Here are Jurassic limestones, 100 million years old; here are oolites – consistent marine sediments made up of numberless tiny balls of calcium rolled into shape by a restless sea.

Coasting from Dorset and then up the Thames into London was a relatively easy journey. As early as 1619, Inigo Jones had specified Portland stone to build Henry VIII's banqueting hall in Whitehall. After the Great Fire, Wren chose it in the great rebuilding – the climax being St Paul's Cathedral constructed in the 1670s. He and Vanburgh alone designed fifty-one churches in Portland stone in London.

Imposing, powerful, dependable, it was the 'natural' stone to use for the Bank of England, the Cenotaph (designed by Lutyens in 1920), Waterloo Bridge rebuilt in 1945 (LCC, Giles Gilbert Scott), and BBC Broadcasting House (1932 and 2012), which carry the high-relief sculptures by Eric Gill. Slivers of stone ashlar were used to cover their facades. It is a wonder that the Isle of Portland still exists, so much has it been pillaged.

In the island's quarries we stared at the stratigraphy of the Portland beds from top to bottom:

Topsoil
Top rubble
Slat
Shingle and clay beds
Bottom rubble
Dirt bed
Top cap
Skull cap
Roach
Whitbed (or white bed)
Perrycot
Basebed (or bestbed)

In the masonry sheds we learned most about the Whitbed. This freestone – meaning it can be cut in any direction – is much sought after, being fine of grain, soft yet durable and of beautiful whiteness. It enabled Eric Gill to make those high-relief sculptures for Broadcasting House.

The Roach beds are full of fossils, making it unreliable, so it's often crushed for road metal, though it has moments of fashion – the Economist Building, the Choir School at St Paul's, and parts of the new BBC building are clad in it – its jumbled, shelly patterns giving texture.

On the island we were able to see all the beds used in every way. As well as field boundaries, you come across paving, kerbs and gutters in worked stone. The rich mix of buildings – cottages, terraces, bridges, walls, as well as the old fort and the big houses – are all made of different Portland beds. The occasional highly desirable fossils of the Whitbed, such as the giant ammonite, *Titanites anguiformis*, three feet in diameter, are embedded in the walls of Easton and Southwell. Roach-bed buildings flaunt Portland screws – *Aptyxiella portlandica* (a turreted gastropod) – and lots more.

We learned much, and glimpses of the deeper culture sometimes shone though: words, names, songs, tools, techniques varying with place. Here on Portland there are still medieval strip fields, gavelkind is practised (the division of wealth and land among all the sons rather than just the firstborn male). Hard physical work, tempered by knowledge gathered over working life, is handed on. Before blasting was commonplace, gangs of four or five men worked along faults freeing the stone from the face using metal wedges, chanting to ensure rhythmic striking by sledgehammers.

Back in London, as well as watching the builders face UCL's front lodges in Portland Whitbed, students saw the repair and restoration of St Mary le Strand (James Gibbs, 1717), where masons frequently found oyster shells originally used to level stones – were they remnants of eighteenth-century lunches? Perhaps one could even trace whose lunch, given that every stone is signed – these mason's marks (crosses, 'v's, reversed letters) were made to ensure that each would receive due payment.

Later in the 1980s, working with Common Ground, we pioneered work helping local people to commission sculpture to celebrate their love of place. On Portland, a sculpture by John Maine takes up the form, found locally, of ancient terraces – strip lynchet – as well as referencing the restless waves. Half an acre of slipping land is made secure by five undulating drystone walls representing Portland beds in stratigraphical turn, each worked and laid in their different traditional ways: Basebed, Whitbed, Roach, Top cap, Slat.

Chiswell Earthworks looks from the West Weares along Chesil Bank and across the sea. It may be massive, but it is a quiet monument, to the extent that people ask: 'Where is the sculpture?' It pays homage to both the limestone and the masons: a powerful exposition of cultural intimacy with the land. It is used for music gatherings, walks, picnics and watching the sunset.

I scan my own horizons now and am glad to have made the acquaintance of limestone. It is a generous stone. The Carboniferous in particular lets one under the surface. Although his heart lay further north than mine, I have to thank W. H. Auden for his words from the end of 'In Praise of Limestone':

> …but when I try to imagine a faultless love
> Or the life to come, what I hear is the murmur
> Of underground streams, what I see is a limestone landscape.

Love of the land offered me an anchor, one that I can use in other places without giving up attachment to my homeground.

I have worked to encourage people to stand up for their everyday surroundings, but I still feel responsible for what we are leaving behind – or rather in front of us. We seem unable to stop ourselves burning what we have dug or sucked from the depths. And our carbon-loaded atmosphere is also affecting our oceans, where limestones begin.

We have changed the air and rain to the extent that even the ocean is 30 percent more acid since we began to industrialise. In only four decades' time that could escalate to 150 percent in ocean acidification. It may be 65 million years since this rate of acidification happened. Already marine creatures are finding it difficult to fix carbon to make shells, coral, bones, and it further debilitates by slowing down their ability to take up oxygen from the water. Add in the stress from the spectrum of contamination we proffer from plastics, chemicals, noise, transport and war.

Of course, time and geology will sort it all out, our 'civilisation' will consolidate into a strange lime-rich layer or two – but what of us in the meantime? What of our fellow creatures and this moment, in a world the like of which we have found nowhere in the universe?

Manifold cycles ever perturbed by butterflies' wings, by the burning of coal. And we are so small, so transient and yet so powerful, so messy, so in need of attachment.

Playing hide-and-seek among stone walls, lying in grass face-to-face with a flower soft and velvet like a bee; leaping incredulously across dry stones where a river should be flowing or standing deep in a dripping cavern singing with glistening towers – knee-deep in memories, it occurs to me that I learned about happiness and freedom, beauty and the land in limestone.

Chalk

WESTBURY

Alyson Hallett

Here's the plan. I'm going to evoke a row of coastguards' cottages near a cliff edge, in Sussex. This is Birling Gap, where the cliffs are made of chalk. These cliffs dissolve into the sea so fast the cottages have to be dismantled. One by one and brick by brick, before they topple over the cliff and onto the beach. Many years ago, I stayed in one of these cottages and remember how precarious it felt being on an edge of land that weakened with each incoming tide. In 2014, even the National Trust surrendered and took down its Birling Gap sun lounge and ice-cream parlour.

Next, we'll go to the Seven Sisters, the White Cliffs of Dover. Ponder the great chalk cliffs of southern England that once joined up with France. Post-Brexit, these cliffs are for me a sign of hope, a flag welcoming anyone who approaches by sea, a reminder that aloneness is an illusion. As the seventeenth-century poet John Donne wrote, 'No man is an island entire of itself; every man is a piece of the continent, a part of the main.' As one pebble is part of the planet, so each person is part of something bigger.

The Channel Tunnel, that great feat of engineering and imagination, joins Britain with mainland Europe. It's an umbilical cord running under the sea, shuttling people back and forth, and all around it the walls are made of chalk. Years ago, as a student, I travelled from Dover to Dunkerque by boat as I headed to Paris to study French. I dreaded those journeys, the rough waves, the sea-sick hours. The arrival of the Eurotunnel was something to celebrate. An underwater handshake that affirms the friendly connections between the UK and elsewhere.

This is a good plan, I thought, solid, reliable – but since when has there been anything in my nature that follows a plan? I'm more like chalk itself – strong and weak, solid and dissolving.

Change comes in the night, when I'm asleep and my head's fast down on a pillow. I dream of a horse galloping across a field. There's a stream of white air around its body, the wind bending to make room for it as it speeds full-pelt from east to west. The question has to be asked – is the spirit of the horse going forth from its body or is the air turning white as it curves around neck and fetlock? Perhaps both, perhaps neither, but what can't be denied is the fact that a thin, whitish line bristles all around the horse, every edge of it, its whole body shimmering.

I wake, filled to the brim with the white horse, its lithe, fast body still cantering through me. This isn't the first time a dream has disrupted my plans – but it's always a surprise and I'm always disbelieving.

An example. In 2001, my grandmother Hilda appeared in a dream and told me to climb Cader Idris, a mountain in the Snowdonia range of North Wales. I ignored her at first – but her voice wouldn't go away, so I gave in and did as I was told. Halfway up the slopes of Cader Idris I met my first erratic, a stone that had travelled in a glacier. I was amazed by this; I'd never heard of a travelling stone before. Weren't stones supposed to be fixed, solid, immobile? Fifteen years later, I'm still running a project called 'The Migration Habits of Stones', still looking at how they move and migrate around the world.

I wish someone at school had told me to take note of my dreams. It could have saved a lot of time and angst. Let's change direction then, away from the cliffs, and towards the White Horse of Westbury.

This horse is emblazoned on a hill just half an hour away from where I live on the edge of the city of Bath. I see the horse most days as I walk back from the bus stop, and I've seen it countless times from the train as it scoots through Wiltshire on its way to London. It's an emblematic beast, a great white beacon pulsing against its entourage of green. On clear days the horse leaps out, a bold and defiant sign. On stormy days it retreats, sinks into the body of itself. On misty days, it disappears altogether.

The White Horse moves and at the same time remains perfectly still. A magic horse. Fixed and in motion, a paradox, a gift, a spell cast in white. Each day it speaks to the earth and speaks to the sky, its body a sign, a muscular language. Imagine that first time when we rode a horse, the deep, intimate contract between rider and steed. We climbed onto a horse's back and galloped from one village to another, we flew, we suddenly knew speeds that made us giddy.

As above, so below, the mystical dictum says, and in the second century, the astronomer Ptolemy named a constellation of stars after Pegasus, the winged horse in Greek mythology. On Earth, we'd already pulled back the scalp of the earth and revealed chalk, a brightness we carved horses out of.

On November 25, I invite Lynn, a friend and poet from New Zealand, to visit the Westbury White Horse with me. She is keen to go on an adventure and so we bundle ourselves into my little gold car and set off. Half an hour later, we're climbing a hill out of Westbury that's so steep I'm in second gear and struggling. Up and up we go into a blue and cloudless sky. I tell Lynn the horse was concreted over in the 1950s, and to my relief she's not too disappointed. As we round a bend on the hill's ridge, Lynn spies a sign for a chalk quarry. I swerve into a lay-by and park. This is where we will begin. In the place where chalk is blasted and sawn from the earth.

Despite the bright sun, the wind is bitter. It bites our hands, our faces, runs its freezing knives through our hair. We wrap up in scarves, hats and gloves, hurry over to the gates at the entrance to the quarry. They're locked. A large, oblong sign declares the name of the cement company that owns it. Of course, you need chalk to make cement, and cement to make concrete – one thing linked up with the other.

I suggest we skirt the perimeter. There's a high, slatted metal fence with an equally high hedge behind it. It's punctuated with warning signs. Each one says, in bright yellow, red, blue and black: *Danger! Quarries are not play areas! Stay Away!*

After a quarter of a mile or so, there's a break in the hedge and we whoop with glee. At last we peer into the quarry. There are three or four pits, each one stepped, as deep as 150 feet. I had no idea the quarry would be this big. Sunlight glances off the sliced, straight faces, and we're curiously silent. There's something eerie about staring into the Earth. As if we're looking into something we shouldn't really see, into the living body of the planet.

The fields around are covered with tiny chalk stones. I pick one up and my fingers whiten. Without thinking, I scratch a line on a rock. It's completely instinctive. Chalk marks me and with chalk I make a mark. I think of my earliest ancestors, the ones who went into the caves of Lascaux and made pictures of running bison, aurochs, ibex. Is this how they started? Chalk is grey and red as well as white. We touch it, and it shows us the potential hidden in its substance, the potential hidden in us.

I rub my fingers together and there's friction, a measure of resistance to the slide of skin against skin. We list the things we learn from this: gymnasts dip their hands in chalk dust before leaping to grasp rings or bars. Rockclimbers reach for chalk to increase their grip, and lessen the likelihood of slippage. I remember Hurricane Higgins, the snooker player I used to watch with my dad, the way he chalked the tip of his cue between shots, something I'd go on to do as a student playing endless games of pool.

Chalk neutralises too – balances acid in soil, gentles an acidic stomach. It prevents silver from tarnishing. Lets a tailor make a mark that can be erased. That disappearing act again – here one minute, gone the next.

A sign, a signal, a flare.

Without chalk, half the buildings that exist wouldn't be there. I wonder why I've never thought about chalk much before now, how I've lived this long without saying thank you for all it does for us.

Chalk begins with plankton. Known as coccolithophores, these one-celled plants like to live in the upper layers of the ocean. Here, they surround themselves with microscopic scales made of lime. These scales are called coccoliths and they're shaped like hubcaps. Unlike hubcaps, they're only three one-thousandths of a millimetre in diameter. When they die, they sink to the bottom of the sea. Skeleton upon skeleton. Until, 35 million years later, heat and pressure transform the sediment into chalk. Flint is nestled in chalk, and if pressure and heat are applied for longer, the seam turns into marble. I stare at the tiny chalk stone in my hand: the line I drew moments ago is not just a line of calcium carbonate – it's the lost language of plankton.

I stumble and fall, wait for a moment before getting up. Then, unselfconsciously, kiss the ground because it's nothing less than miraculous.

Wheatears and sparrows serenade us as we stumble on from the quarry to the horse. The sun is fierce and bright, and Wiltshire spreads for hundreds of miles beneath us. Hay bales in fields look like notes on a stave, although Lynn thinks they're more like Braille. Far away, the Mendip Hills undulate.

We turn a corner and suddenly, there it is. Huge and white, head, ear, eye, tail, rump, its whole bright body blazing on a slope so steep it makes me giddy. We try to take it in. The horse swoops down, ultra-white against the emerald green of winter grass. I forget to breathe. I had no idea that it would be this big, this bold, unlike anything I've ever seen. Lynn says how much courage it must have taken to make it, to hack into a hill that is vertiginous.

The Westbury Horse is the only chalk horse that stands still: legs straight, hooves planted in earth, as stony and meditative as horses are sometimes inclined to be. At the same time there's nothing fixed about it, nothing that makes me think it couldn't change its mind and gallop off across the fields.

The nearest part of the horse to the path is its ear. I touch it, then tentatively inch down to the place where its nostrils would be. I pause before easing myself into the horse's mouth.

Instantly, the wind stops.

The horse is dug a foot or so into the hill and this depth protects me. I stretch out, lay flat against the white concrete. 'You okay down there?' Lynn shouts. 'Fine,' I call back. Below, a few cars beetle along a road, a concrete factory repeatedly thumps, a train speeds by on its way to London. I wonder if the passengers can see me – then realise how unlikely that is. I am less than a speck in the horse's mouth, barely the size of a tooth.

I clamber back up. The horse's eye is made of black bricks arranged in a herringbone pattern. As many as one hundred and fifty, if not more. Curved and beautiful, the eye anchors the horse to earth.

During the Second World War, people hid the horse beneath brushwood and turf so that enemy aircraft couldn't use it as a landmark. Then, like a phoenix, it rose again. The earliest record of the horse is on a map in 1773, but the need to create chalk figures is much older than that. The naked giant of Cerne Abbas, who wields a club and sports an enormous erection, was made circa 1650. The

White Horse of Uffington is much older. It was created 3,000 years ago, in the late Bronze Age.

It has been in our pagan blood for a long time then, this need to make pictures with chalk – to extend beyond the limits of our bodies. A building, a line, a cross – Hindu sacred symbols chalked on doorsteps, protective circles chalked by witches, the chalk blessing of a Christian epiphany. Artists have chalked Mona Lisa onto pavements; Einstein arrived at $E=mc^2$ with chalk; its white tongue showed many of our grandparents their nine times tables. Who would have thought that for so much of our lives we have been collaborating with plankton? That each time a child draws a hopscotch grid, they're doing it with the assistance of something that's taken millions of years to create?

Lynn and I head off for lunch and stumble across a farm shop and café in Edington, where I tuck into roasted parsnip soup and Lynn munches her way through a chicken and chorizo pie. After coffee and a shared slice of banana, maple and pecan cake, we brace the searing wind and return to the horse.

Fresh molehills freckle the ground, each one dotted with small stones. I wonder if the moles acquire white stripes when they burrow through chalk. Zebra moles, Lynn says. It is half past three, and our shadows are nearly as long as they can be. Wintering trees in the valley catch fire – umber, ochre, vermilion. A thin mist drifts across the valley, smoke ribbons out from chimneys. As the sun withdraws, the temperature drops and Lynn scurries back to the car.

The horse's pelt is pinkish now, the sun its couturier as Earth notches up another degree of elliptical orbit. The roads of the world turn dark. *Goodbye, horse.* I touch its ear one last time, squirrel three stones in my pocket and head for home.

Flint

ALDERLEY EDGE

Alan Garner

Flint.

Listen.

I go to let the hens out before breakfast. Three fields away the dish and antenna of the Lovell Telescope at Jodrell Bank wait to hear something that once happened.

The hens tumble from their hut to drink. One scratches for a worm. And something glints in the scratching, catching the sun. I pick it up and hold it, a stone, a wonder, in my hand. I know what this is; and I'm the first to know in the 10,000 years since the last hand that held it. And that hand and mine just could be linked.

I lift the stone against the light. It's thin, translucent, honey-black and sharp; sharper than a surgeon's steel; and in it, as if in amber, a fossil, a frond of a creature from the sea.

Back at the house for breakfast, I spoon muesli with one hand, and with the other turn the shining thing. It fits my fingers.

Two strikes made it; broke it free; and a bone pressed it to perfect the edge. Ten thousand years ago.

Someone brought it here. There's no flint in Cheshire. After the ice, people walked from Europe, following the herds. The flint was in Yorkshire. It passed from hand to hand around camp fires, a chalky lump, until it reached where the garden is now. A blow hit the lump, and the honey-black shone.

The spur of land sits above the valley, with water on three sides, and well-drained soil; a good winter camp for hunter-gatherers, and a time for mending and making, telling stories, watching for the game to come down to drink. Then skinning the flesh of the kill.

The postman drives up the track into the yard. I slit the envelope with the flint. Inside is the result of the radiocarbon dating of a cremation we disturbed at the corner of the house. The figure is 1,387 plus or minus 29 BP, which means 3,500 years ago, give or take. The house is on a Bronze Age barrow. And though the house is 500 years old and more, it's not the first. There are at least two others beneath; with roundhuts under the garden and the yard. The people who came here after the ice did not go away. Why move when you find the place ideal?

> A quarter of a million fires
> Have been on this hearth;
> The hearth in the house
> Where the days have seen
> Hall and hut over the burnt dead.
> Across the field, the telescope
> Has news. A star flares
> In Cygnus. I look
> So far away the star had died
> Before the grave was born.

And what about the flint? How did that happen?

There was a warm sea over England, and in it were plankton and snails. They died; and their scales and shells drifted down and settled on the sea floor. They built the chalk more than half a kilometre thick.

But a kilometre is a cold measure. I can't understand a length that is based on one ten-millionth of the distance from the Equator to the pole. My mind is one of miles. A mile is a measure of the body; a pace, a fifteen-minute walk. It's the measure that brought us out of Africa with a stone in our hand.

The weight of half a mile of chalk pressed the silica of the shells and scales. Larger creatures burrowed through the ooze, and the silica followed, filling the tunnels and burrows; settled, and was hard, a cast of where they'd been.

The world heaved, the chalk weathered, and the silica was flint. Inside its grey husk it grew beauty, waiting to be got.

My blood walked out of Africa 90,000 years ago. We came by flint. Flint makes and kills; gives shelter, food; it clothes us. Flint clears forest. Flint brings fire. With flint we bear the cold.

Listen.

What is this that is coming?

Listen.

A heart-shaped pebble, worn by water, lies in a shallow brook. A hand takes it.

The pebble fits the hand. It's hard and black and good. But it can be better. It can be made better. The mind sees how; and the other hand strikes with another stone. It knocks flakes from one side of the black, each flake drawing sparks into a sharp and wavy edge. The point of the heart is hit more gently to whittle slivers; and the work is done.

Now the pebble is an axe in the hand, to butcher with. The edge cuts hide and flesh and sinew and opens up the marrow of a bone. The point digs between and prises limbs apart.

What is this that is coming?

Mervyn stands by the belt on the tractor as the potatoes are lifted from the field. He picks off the rubbish. The tractor passes over the pond that the motorway men filled with their spoil when they made the cutting. The earth is claggy and yellow, not loam, and there are more stones than spuds. He throws the stones back to the field.

He takes one to sling; and stops. It's black, and it sits in his hand, just right. It's small and smooth, but jagged on one side and pointed at the end. The stone gleams, and there is light inside.

Mervyn puts the stone in his pocket, and on his way home he drops it off at the house on the hill.

I sit in the old house on the ancient mound and read the County Archaeologist's notes.

'Site. A reclaimed marl-pit at Grid Reference SJ 77/744755 filled with spoil from a cutting on the M6.

Description. The artefact is a pebble of black flint, with smooth, natural facets and naturally rounded butt, all showing derived features. The end is pointed, and on one side a sinuous edge has been formed by bifacial chipping and step-flaking to give a triangular section. The other side has been heavily blunted.

Remarks. On the superficial evidence, it would appear to be a Lower Palaeolithic handaxe, preserved from destruction under the Anglian and subsequent glaciations. It is Abbevillean in execution.'

I sit back. Abbevillean. That's more than six Ice Ages ago. It must be half a million years. How did it survive?

Half a million. It wasn't *Homo sapiens*. *Homo erectus*, perhaps. Or *Homo heidelbergensis*. Or some such. And now in my hand.

I look out of the window at the telescope. The dish is tilted. The antenna is collecting signals so faint that they have to be cooled to near absolute zero to steady the atoms before the data can be sent to the computers.

A light, not thought, flashes in my brain.

I log on to the telescope to find what it's hearing. It's a quasar, a mass of energy with a black hole at its centre swallowing stars; near the beginning of Time, more than 13,000 million light years away, more than 13,000 million years ago; before our solar system was formed; before our galaxy took shape. And the whispers of that energy, travelling at the speed of light, about 180,000 miles a second, seven times around the world in a second, one and a quarter seconds to the Moon, eight minutes to the Sun, four point two years to the nearest star, two point five million to the nearest galaxy like ours – the whispers are arriving at the antenna of the telescope Now; if Now exists; if Now is possible. And I sit with the axe in my hand.

The axe is a first meddling with the Universe by our intelligence. Intelligence took what was and changed it, to make it work better. Once that has happened, the telescope becomes inevitable. Idea leads to idea in a chain reaction of discovery that won't be stopped. Eve will pick the apple. Pandora cannot shut the box. We are the questing ape: the ape that says, 'What's next?'

The pebble opens the Cosmos. If mind had not interfered with pebble, if hand had not struck flake, no dish would hear, and no antenna focus.

Half a million years. Thirteen thousand million years.

When the hand picked the pebble to fetch the telescope, the whispers had covered more than ninety-seven percent of their journey to this Cheshire field. And I hold the flint, full of stars. And wonder.

The pebble opens the Cosmos. And yet, lost in the immensity of understanding, should I not fear this thing?

> Forwards to the power of ten to the Sun's nova.
> And beyond that.
> Backwards, Time lies bedded
> Stripped by the wind, made again,
> And a new Time to be
> Stripped by the wind.
> The rain grates mountains
> That were over Snowdon
> That were under seas.
> And beyond that.

All Time bears on a single moment.
The one point of light is
Intolerable.

'Of Abbevillean execution', says the note. The axe is named from the place where its type was first identified. Intelligence shaped it. But is intelligence enough to save us from ourselves? And are we, alone, intelligent in this vastitude? There's an argument that says it may be that we have not yet found intelligence beyond our world because intelligence that evolves to be conscious of itself carries within its own destruction. So will the flint that shaped us be our nemesis, our nemesis of Abbevillean execution?

We've been here before. We've had practice. We have rehearsed. Abbeville is in the valley of the Somme.

Gypsum and Alabaster

BRANSCOMBE AND RIPON

Rose Ferraby

In early January 2014, a storm swept the coastline of south-west England. Giant waves cruised in, slapping the cliffs, clawing rocky crevasses. As the storm raged one night, I walked down to the beach at Branscombe in East Devon. The darkness was filled with the hiss and suck of waves towing pebbles back to the deep. The beach quivered under the force of the sea. The next morning, in the calm that followed, the beach looked very different. A whole new stratigraphy at the cliff base had been exposed: a new-born stretch of pristine red mudstone, vivid in the sunshine. And weaving through it, a band of glistening something, threading through the cliff as though it were holding it together like a geological corset. Gypsum. The pale crystal threads sparkled and rippled beneath a cascade of water fleeing the cliff. This was my first sight of gypsum: a strange, wraithlike substance, hiding in plain sight.

As an archaeologist, I'm very used to furtling in the ground. My eyes have adapted to the colour palette, textures, sounds and structures that link the surface with underground worlds. Past encounters with stone have come from cutting sonorous letters into limestone, exploring underground mines or quarries on a fellside, reading past activity in marked forms. I feel on safe ground with the key stones: the granites, limestones, sandstones and such like, which form such a grand part of my own cultural geology. But gypsum, gypsum is something quite different. It is present but we don't really see it; it is old-fashioned yet up-to-the-mark. Gypsum exists in our lives secretively, we encounter it every day: it makes the plasterboard that divides up our houses and offices – a shield resistant to flame. It is used as fertilizer on fields to grow our food, and in our toothpaste. Gypsum is also found on Mars in a faint echo of watery life, and was used to build the great pyramids of Egypt; so much part of our daily lives, yet simultaneously distant in time and space. It can be powdered up or can loom huge, like the fifty-foot-long crystals in a mine in Mexico. These scales of connection can be hard to grasp, yet on closer acquaintance gypsum has real charm and a wonderful lithological poetry to it. It goes beyond just being a stone in the straightforward sense of being solid and impenetrable. Rather, it is a stone that is also mutable; that is characterised by absence and light as much as by physical presence. I've found the cultural and geological narratives that dwell within it to be surprising, and enchanting.

Gypsum is a relatively common stone worldwide, often lurking between other beds of stone, or creeping its way in through fissures and faults. As a result, it can be found in big beds that are easily quarried, or in veins and nodules. It is almost jewel-like in its variable transparency, displaying hues of white, pale creams, sienna and rust. At my local museum, a glass case displays a few fragments alongside more colourful, blingy bits and bobs. A long, white form with myriad bevels resembles a strip light. Another shows its crystalline character in a cluster of growing fronds, frozen in time in their heritage display. The geometric growths have been stunted, but left alone in the earth these continue to grow and spread. I can only imagine the feel of its solid mineral bulk. I long to touch: is it smooth like a snake, mirroring its slithering subterranean wanderings? Or, like a shark, does its visible smoothness contrast with a rough, sandpaper stroke?

Geologically, gypsum is a slippery customer to get the hang of. And this is because of its ability to change rapidly as it comes into, or lacks, contact with water. It is a soluble rock, dissolving at a rate somewhere between limestone and salt. To begin with, gypsum forms in shallow, enclosed seas as calcium sulphate combined with water. As the water evaporates, rock and mineral deposits are left behind, like the saltpans of Utah or Bolivia that we see today. The process of gradual geological burial to depths greater than 3,000 feet and temperatures more than 42°C forces it to become dehydrated, and it loses volume. It becomes anhydrite: calcium sulphate without the water. Over thousands of years, these beds can be uplifted. When they are within 300 feet or so of the surface once more, they can come into contact with groundwater, rehydrating and regaining volume to become secondary gypsum or alabaster.

But this is not the end of the story. Contact with water continues to control the behaviour of gypsum. It appears and disappears, at speeds that are more on a human timescale than a geological one. The energy of movement can affect its form. The water that combines with it takes on powers of petrification. Water and gypsum are in a constant dance: drawing away, coming together; the gypsum dissolving or solidifying at the touch of hydration. As a result, this curious stone flows invisible beneath us, transient and pale. We rarely find outcrops of it, as it dissolves away too rapidly. Instead we become aware of it if it is suddenly exposed in a cliff, down in a quarry, or in its absence as it leaves a sinkhole in the earth. Brief glimpses of a secret geological life.

At Branscombe, the gypsum threads through the mudstone in pale, shining veins. Its exposure brought to light part of its human, as well as its geological, history. One of gypsum's most common uses is in the creation of Plaster of Paris, when its powdered, dehydrated form is mixed with water to make it pliable before setting hard. The 'of Paris' is a distant echo of the quarries that once littered Montmartre; exploited gypsum beds leaving the modern city precarious. It was extracted at Branscombe in the fourteenth century to be used in the cathedral at Exeter. In a mass migration of stone from this area, gypsum accompanied the local dimension limestone's whose geological beds were taken out of twist and chiselled into regular blocks, quoins and gargoyles. As the huge building rose in the city, it became a rearranged stratigraphy of local geology. And sealing it all, the Plaster of Paris; minute fragments of those gypsum threads spread white from the limestone floor to the arching heights of the ceiling. In some areas of the cathedral, the plaster forms the base layer for colourful murals. In others, the white finish reflects light back and forth between those high walls and stained-glass windows.

The light catches on objects collected and cherished around floor level. In many cathedrals and churches we see effigies, altarpieces and figures whose stone seems to glow pale and wan. This is gypsum in another form: alabaster. Its complex crystals give translucence, traced here and there with ferrous veins or stroked with an orange hue. The light catches and holds in the heart of the stone. In some buildings it has been sliced fine and thin to be used at the windows; sunlight refracting in a subterranean glow. This earth-aged, rehydrated gypsum is soft to carve into. No heavy tools are required – you can even use your nail, like a cuttlefish bone from the beach. Alabaster was often used as an alternative to marble, allowing complex scenes to be portrayed in detail. Look carefully and we see the textures of the cloth on a woman's cloak, the fall of a man's beard, expressions alive and present in faces. Some were painted, but for many it was the play of light through the stone which really brought soul to these pieces: a warm glow amid everyday medieval life. The flat alabaster was a canvas into which generations of names were cut and actions venerated to be held in the palm of the stone. But before ecclesiastical spires erupted from the British landscape, alabaster was already a memory-maker: at one site, archaeologists found a Roman sepulchral urn. It held close the material scatters of a past life – ash, lead, pot – the stone aglow in the earth despite its reburial.

There is an uncanny resonance between gypsum – this secretive stone – and the ways in which we have tried to capture fleeting human lives; to extend our memories of them into the reassurance of geological endurance. Back in the museum cabinet, alongside the pale lumps of gypsum, was a plaster cast of a trilobite. The ancient rippled body of what looked like a marine woodlouse, that roamed the world's oceans for over 270 million years. I was struck by this little cast. It was a solid form of an empty space. The material echo of a distant death.

The trilobite led me to think about other ways of casting bodies, histories and lives. When excavating Pompeii in the nineteenth century, archaeologists realised that the ghostly spaces of bodies were preserved in the solid ash. They poured Plaster of Paris into these voids to create casts, resurrecting the disappeared dead from their hollows. The plaster crept into nooks and crannies, revealing odd features of faces and clothing – a far cry from those detailed etchings in alabaster. The cast of a dog shows the leashed animal squirming to escape, its teeth bared, fur ruffled. These plaster figures are displayed on site and in museums, so the modern public can feel a far-off echo of the volcanic end of those Roman lives. You can't help but be moved by them. They have captured not only a body, but an energy of a town being smothered, a moment of breath held, time halted. There is, however, a sense of shame in looking at them, as they are displayed like objects, not people. The plaster, solidifying air, plays with the idea of the form – it is at once a body and a sculpture. It is fossilising memory and time. In her cast sculptures of buildings, the artist Rachel Whiteread describes this as 'mummifying the air in the room'. The time-travelling gypsum has been used to capture a stir of the past, giving a solid tool with which to imagine the unimaginable.

The mutable gypsum tide turns, and we move from its materiality to its absence.

Where in one place material builds, it leaves a void elsewhere. What of gypsum's negative spaces? Out in the landscape we find the pale hollows of gypsum extraction. The area around Nottingham was once famed for its alabaster industry, the beds nibbled back as carved forms were traded out and away. As fashions changed, the old quarries went quiet. We see faint traced echoes of them in the land: the forms of old mines, overgrown railway tracks and tantalising blocked entrances. One abandoned gypsum mine at Fauld in Staffordshire found its earlier story rudely erased. The pillar-and-post method of excavation, which had styled the mine's subterranean architecture, made it the perfect place for storing munitions during the Second World War. But on the morning of November 27, 1944, an accident at the site caused the largest explosion on UK soil. It was heard and felt for miles, and in its wake a gaping crater stands as a memorial, shattering the neat field systems and dwarfing the trees.

Further north along this soluble, geological spine of England lies the city of Ripon. This is my home country, where for me the Anglo-Saxon foundations of the cathedral, the Victorian spa baths and market town hold a sense of enduring history. I can trace faint glimmers of archaeology here. But under all this, a greater excavator lurks. Beneath the superficial bedrocks of Ripon, a bed of gypsum lies. Caves and breccia pipes form voids and points of weakness. As water travels through the different beds, an alchemy of dissolution leaves the earth above unstable, hovering. Until, *schwumph*. The surface is plunged down into a sinkhole. Ripon is getting quite a reputation for these hollow surprises.

The geological slumpings can begin slowly. Cracks might creep through a house and garden, levels gradually finding less in common until the buildings begin to sheer and droop. Other sinkholes happen rapidly, huge craters appearing in fields, streets or back gardens, as though a giant worm had just turned on its heel. The craters left in the urban surface are a spooky entrance to the underworld; a gaping void exposing the normally unnoticed geology. They bring with them a sense of fear, a vivid image of what it would be like to be consumed by the earth. They create strange phenomena: smells of sulphur, or a mighty draught like the stony deep breath of a sleeping giant. It is not surprising then to find out that they harbour their own myths and are wrapped into stories. It is thought that the gypsum-generated gulfs in Ripon might have inspired Lewis Carroll when he wrote *Alice in Wonderland*: 'I wonder if I shall fall right through the earth?' thinks Alice as she plunges down. Carroll's father lived in Ripon, and many such holes were recorded in the years before he wrote the book; might the Mad Hatter be lurking below?

In recent years, geologists have brought to us their own narrative gems, creating cartographies of Ripon's mutable nether-regions. We see familiar markers from the human world overwritten by numbers flagging the levels of subsidence. Another map shows the dates of sinkholes. Some spots, particular streets, are repeat victims. Magdalen Road is one such, its gardens, outhouses and side streets picked off slowly through the years. A pattern has emerged of linear cracks below the surface: a joint controlled cave system in the gypsum, stark reminders of the metamorphic nature of this strange stone. We are learning more about the strange ways of gypsum each year, as geologists zoom in and out from its underground cartographies to its inner crystalline make-up seen in thin section.

Stone needs a period of acquaintance. You have to get to know its unique character, its life history. Gypsum can be difficult to get to know. Geological descriptions of it are hard to grasp, the language of science sometimes rendering its mutable properties indecipherable. But I have unexpectedly found stories of it in familiar places. Its presence has grown in my perception of landscape both outdoors and in. It is a stone defined by its reaction with water, this interplay creating forms of presence and absence that have entered our daily lives in myriad ways. It is a fleeting memory in and of itself.

At Branscombe, the beach has since returned. On a pebbled walk there recently, I went in search of those tendrils of gypsum. But they had gone, vanished again like a subterranean creature. Until the next storm.

Clay Bricks

BRISTOL

Fiona Hamilton

Walking along Clay Pit Road, Bristol, in the rain, I feel the earth squelchy under my feet, waterlogged and soft. Clay was dug up here for a hundred or so years and fed the local brick industry. That clay pit may even have been the source of the red bricks that make up the terraced house I've just moved into. It was constructed in 1900 by builders who also built the nearby railway arches and tunnels. I'm thinking about this journey of clay to brick, with its alchemy, its economies, and its repercussions for how we live now.

Inside the house, it's warm. I've been cleaning the bricks around the fireplace with vinegar solution and a wire brush. Their orangey-red has emerged from under a dark patina. I've rubbed around the mortar, having read that mortar is not so much glue as a cushion. Bricks move and breathe. Mortar, especially a hundred-odd years ago, was lime-based and soft. The bricks' hue is warm, soft-warm, deep-warm, like the sound of a cello, like fire that has had time to settle and get to know itself, to acquire deeper russets and golds, fire that has moved beyond sparks and showy pyrotechnics. This red brick is familiar, old, resonant. It's comforting.

The bricks have textures – some are grainy, others smoother. I run my fingers over them, wanting to be connected to a process of making, remaking, grateful for these solid un-showy things that can be held in my hand, grateful that they have not crumbled, though walls surely can. Older bricks are solid but not weather-proof: rain can get in and frost can cause them to spall. A storm blew through my life and my family's and I am propelled by some kind of instinct to rebuild, even though I know that re-building is a kind of oxymoron. We can only build, and, if we choose, bring into the building something good, salvaged and authentic, hoping for warmth, a breath of life, whatever form that takes.

And so I start to ask questions. What are these unitary, indistinguishable little blocks that I have taken for granted, that I am now, for the first time, washing, almost caressing, as if they are precious, rare things? Is it their ordinariness that is comforting me? Is it that they are the product of the earth, moulded by humans?

Thus begins a trail, a quest of sorts, back in time to the pre-history of the brick, and through the streets of Bristol which, like so many British cities, is built of brick. The clay pits that supplied the raw material across England were located particularly in the south and east. In East Anglia, where melted ice had left abundant boulder clay, the land was rich and potent with possibilities that would be explored and exploited by humans over centuries as they investigated its adaptable and perhaps alchemical capabilities. Farmers would pasture cattle on its soft terrain. When they had learned how to 'marl' the clay with limey, chalky and sandy soils to break it down and make its fertile components more accessible for plants and crops, they would concentrate on growing wheat and other crops. They would come to understand that fire could turn clay into another useful form. After the enclosures of common land in the eighteenth century, many farmers realised that the value of their land was underneath as well as on top – clay not hay.

Brickmaking could be combined with sheep-rearing and crop-growing, for the cycles of these different seasonal activities complemented each other. Clay was dug in the autumn, weathered over the winter. Moulding began when danger of frost was over, after sowing and lambing. The kiln was kept ablaze from April to November. In a symbiotic arrangement, the tile and brick industry expanded in concert with the building of transport links, and the acceleration of house building.

Where would our cities be without brick? Resilient, seemingly democratic, with wide appeal, a material that is tough yet aesthetic, that finds new uses in old skin. But I want to go further back in time, to explore the beginnings, the original clay. That earth can be baked hard by the sun was discovered millennia ago. Somehow, even before the contemporary scientists who are investigating 'hydrogels' – microscopic pockets within clay where biochemical reactions can happen that produce proteins, new life forms – humans had a feeling that this grey-brown sludge-stuff was potent.

Myths of human beings being formed out of clay exist in multiple traditions and cultures, including Greek, Christian, Islamic, Yoruba, Mayan and Maori. Prometheus's fire warmed cool clay into life and created humans. Clay's inchoate fertile promise seems to invite stories, and acts, of creation.

In the beginning, there was rock. Weathered, pulverised and sifted over billions of years, its particles formed in the presence of ice and water. As ice sheets edged their way south, a thick layer of boulder clay was left in their wake. Minerals travelled down rivers, coming to rest somewhere flat, somewhere near the surface of the earth. Clay, malleable, waterlogged, impermeable, formed. Composed of millions of particles, it accumulated under pastures and flatlands, where birds, animals, insects and plant life made their homes, through the recurring seasons, for millennia.

And then. The intervention of humans with tools, and fire. Ready to unearth, literally, ways that clay could turn into its opposite. They would find out how it could be made to transform, permanently, from something wet and soft to something dry and strong.

The molecular changes to clay would be explained later, much later, but the instinct was there already – this stuff, we had a hunch, could be pulled out of the ground and be made to grow tall. It could stand higher and live longer than humans. With the assistance of fire, it could do magical things.

The average life span of a brick is 500 years. The word 'brick' itself has continuity, remaining relatively unchanged through Germanic, Dutch and French versions since medieval times, with only a few letters' and slight pronunciation differences. The no-nonsense, unadorned single syllable seems at one with the object, as if word and thing were fused together in an inalterable bond that, like brick itself, won't come undone except in temperatures of over 2000°C. I like finding other one-syllabled words that cluster around the brick. They feel like graspable units, solid. A 'hod' means, originally, 'a basket for carrying earth'. The indentation in the top of a brick is called a 'frog' because of the appearance of the mould that made it. So – a hod carries a brick. A brick has a frog.

A word carries meaning. A metaphor means carrying across – one thing allied with another. We shape your world, say the bricks, and the words. And you shape us.

Time and energy are compressed into these blocks, and I am becoming aware of their potency, packed with meaning and history. I wonder if they hold a residual memory right back to their pre-existence as clay, soaked into softness, sifted and sieved by the long journey with the glaciers, and down rivers.

The burr of a passing train brings me to the present and reminds me of the relationship of railways with the brick industry. The development of steam trains and associated technologies posed the problem of how to get trains running over the country's uneven terrain. Twenty thousand miles of tracks and viaducts was the answer, formed with millions of bricks. Wanted: itinerant brickworkers who would travel the country and live in huts on-site. This was hungry work – kilns needed stoking twenty-four hours a day. I imagine lines of railway track being rolled out yard by yard, trains inching along them across the country, bringing coal to fuel kilns that in turn create the brick to create more track. The inexorable clatter of progress.

Brick – the tangible currency of industrialisation. Tradeable, unitary, replicated. Robust. Fickle. Stacked and mass-produced. Hold a brick in your hand and it will speak to you of the troubling god of progress. The hand-made, the home-spun, bows to *more* and *quicker*; imperfections and charm fall away, and work is about serving the self-perpetuating process of growth. Bricks become both products and producers of a sped-up, steamed-up, smoke-belching environment. Red bricks for railways, lines of workers' terraced houses, future factories. Hull, Manchester, Leeds, cities and towns all across England altered their sub-structures, infrastructures and fundamental appearance to serve production – textiles, locomotive parts, or bricks themselves. A seemingly endless input-output loop, generating something better, faster and more. From Spinning Jenny, to spinning train wheels, to spinning textile mills, the pace accelerates and the spin-offs – pollution, stress, unemployment – are mere afterthoughts. The same Victorian bricks stand and quietly observe as our twenty-first-century inheritance is recast. A reclaimed warehouse becomes a sleek high-tech space for digital web-weavers working all hours. A nightclub in an old sugar mill has forgotten that its origins are clay from the nearby riverbed: it is glittering and non-stop, and its developers are making an empire.

And so the brick reinvents itself. Here it is in walls, buildings, stations, schools, houses, flats, arches, tunnels, factories, warehouses, chimneys, stadiums. Each a symphony of substances and reactions that have travelled out of the silty edges of riverbeds where they started as amorphous, malleable earth. Lifted, sifted, dried, moulded. Curves made into lines. Expensive, cheap, sought-after, ugly, attractive, intricate, utilitarian, it is weathered maybe, but not bothered.

Between one-half and two-thirds of the world's population live or work in buildings made with brick clay. We can trace this durable relationship from adobe-mud brick-makers in Turkey in 7000 BC and wall paintings in Thebes showing Ancient Egyptians carrying clay for sun-dried brick. The size, shape and colour of bricks give clues to the architectural historian. The Romans, who brought mobile kilns and spread brick-making throughout their empire, produced squarer and shallower bricks than we are used to. After they left there was a 700-year lull until brick-making began to revive with influences from the Low Countries, and then Flemish brick-makers settled in England, bringing skills and designs.

The names of bricks indicate varieties of shape: bullnose, channel, coping, cownose, hollow. They come in an array of colours, which arise from the components of their originating clay, from the temperature they are fired at, and sometimes from artificial tinting and colouring. Iron-rich clay brings out the red. Lime in clay gives a golden tone. Manganese brings out grey-light-brown tones, and cobalt, blue. The presence of carbonate minerals, such as calcite and dolomite, can produce paler-coloured bricks. Yellow 'London stocks', made from a mixture of clay and calcium carbonate (chalk), were replaced by red bricks from clay further north as the century went on and transportation became easier. Some bricks acquired equally colourful names, such as 'Accrington bloods'. They're as robust as they sound and will last forever, I'm told.

Christopher Wren insisted that the re-building of London inside the city walls after the Great Fire should be done in brick. But making it was smelly, dirty and costly. Chimneys and kilns have belched smoke into the air to produce it over centuries. Bricks are fired at between 900 and 1200°C. Too long or too hot and clay melts. Not long enough and it is fragile. Having undergone this transmutation by fire, the rock-like durable slabs are fire-resistant.

The brick industry is energy-intensive; in recent years the climate-change levy has encouraged energy-saving measures which affect it. Its carbon dioxide is in the fuel used to manufacture the product and from the carbonate minerals in the raw materials. For some products with high carbonate contents, carbon dioxide emissions from the clay body may be as much as from the fuel used for firing.

And what of the human costs? Brick kilns in India employ more than 23 million workers, many of whom migrate for work from other states. Where there is debt-bondage children also work and cannot attend school. Anti-slavery oganisations campaign to improve conditions and introduce policies ensuring that children of brick-kiln workers go to primary school. What is a brick's value to a child pummelling earth in a developing country?

When I lit the fire in this fireplace for the first time in the autumn I attended to this thought, and the people who continue to bear the brunt of making bricks for mass production in a speeded-up world. I can't solve their problems on my own but perhaps bricks, rather than representing walling off or protectionism, can be reminders of uniqueness, solidarity and collaboration.

If clay evokes feminine dimensions of pre-birth, womb, amniotic dreaming, the within and the below, I am familiar with these. And if the brick under my hands makes me see the masculine, my father's hands in mine, essential tools of my daily activities, I appreciate this, too. Bricks are fundamental blocks of our environment. Easy to overlook. Numerous, repeating, apparently similar, but on closer inspection varied and intricate. They are travellers through geological and human time. Intimate with societies and changing human tastes and technologies. And also elemental forms born of earth, water, air and fire.

My Rock

SOUTHMEAD HOSPITAL

Tim Dee

In late August 2017, I was admitted to hospital in Bristol as an emergency patient. Although I could walk from my home to the ambulance in the street outside, and the attending paramedics drove at what they called 'road speed' without using their siren, I was closer to death than I have ever been. I had developed sepsis behind an infection caused by a kidney stone. Two days earlier I had woken with a hot ache at the right side of the base of my back. When the ambulance delivered me to the A & E department, a consultant came to my bed. By then, he said, as he drew black arrows on my abdomen with a marker pen, I was 'falling off a cliff'.

Stone rhymes with bone. And the months of sickness that followed – between a first operation to by-pass my dangerous rock, and, then, a second to remove it – gave me time (feverish at first, enfeebled later, convalescent on a sofa later still) to discover something of my own inner geology, a living landscape, and, having somehow taken a stone *inside*, to think about what it might mean to have internalised geology.

★

Fifteen years ago, I often listened to *Steve Wright's Sunday Love Songs* on BBC Radio 2. The network describes it as 'a blend of classic love songs, dedications and real-life romance stories.' I am not especially soppy, but at that time something of the show's mix hit home. My heart wasn't so happy or made up then – my house seemed built on sand – and every week I totted up the number of times a dedicated song came with a description of the dedicatee as the 'rock' of the dedicator. Some weeks we made double figures.

I'd like to dedicate this song to my rock, and to two experts in demolition, Mr Koupparis and Mr Timoney, of North Bristol NHS Trust.

My first operation stopped the stone in its tracks. In my right kidney – its birthplace and residence – it had grown too bulky to go anywhere else, but was knocking at the exit. Stones over 5 millimetres in diameter are thought mostly too big to pass. Mine was measured at 6. Mr Koupparis inserted a stent – a 250-millimetre-long plastic tube passed up the pipe of my penis – that effectively sidelined the stone and let my kidney drain urine down my ureter as it ought into my bladder. The stent remained *in situ* for twelve weeks and my 'chaotic blood' calmed, at least for a time.

I was *occupied* for months: immobilised by my stone and almost continually aware of it; rescued by the stent, but then injured by it as it outstayed its welcome and turned against me with disabling pain. I came to both fear and to love that word 'pass', with its suggestion of traffic and of camouflage. Inside myself, I had grown a new feature. Here was a novelty item in my own grotto. But, unlike most of its solid surroundings, my stone was mobile; and furthermore, my body knew it as an erratic and wanted it out.

Won't you roll away the stone?

To pass a stone for a man (men are rocked more often than women) can mean to roll it from kidney to bladder, or from bladder to urethra, or from within your penis until, at journey's end, it falls out. The colic or pain of such a passage is famous for being bad. It has been measured; often only childbirth is said to beat it. Similarly, a rock might be moved through a glacier and jettisoned. Only poets have guessed at the Weltschmerz that it might prompt. As the doctors discussed my passing chances, I thought of the lead-shot from a wildfowler's gun that I spat once from a mouthful of goose meat onto an enamel plate. There, it zinged like a ball finding its place on a roulette wheel.

In hospital, I was often asked to rank my pain on a scale of one – not so bad – to ten – deadly. I answered, thinking of the Avon Gorge near my home, its savage gash of limestone perpetually wounded by a muddy river. The rock routes undertaken by cliff climbers there, as elsewhere, have been adjectivally graded – easy, moderate, difficult, hard difficult, very difficult, hard very difficult, severe, hard severe, hard very severe, and extremely severe. There was a guide – though I was never a climber, I have a copy somewhere in my bat cave of books – whose title I've carried with me for decades. It was called 'Extremely Severe in the Avon Gorge'.

An un-passable stone, buried within a cage of flesh and bone, will linger. It might shift within, but may not appear until either the carcass disappears from around it, like a melted glacier, or it is otherwise removed from the stricken body, like a quarried item. Our species has suffered rocks for ages. We've been stone-formers throughout our own geological epoch. A bladder stone, found in 1901, in an Egyptian mummy was dated to 4800 BC. Thus laden, we have long sought remedies. Surgery to treat kidney stones was first described in the eighth century BC in India.

> And, behold, there was a great earthquake: for the angel of the Lord descended from heaven, and came and rolled back the stone from the door, and sat upon it.

My stone festered as it waited. Or rather it caused my waste and grot, whose egress it blocked, to fester behind it. On its own, I think, a stone might be innocent, but it had so grown that, as well as allowing filth to bloom, it could only hurt what it touched or moved against, its home. In hospital, I had various CT (computed tomography) scans: screen grabs of meat bingo played in my septic tank. Among the slices of old mortadella was a moony white shape, pin-ball round and gun-pellet hard, apparently alive, wounding my lights and melts and offal, hurting my softness with its dense intelligence. The image I saw was as close as I have seen to my British Geological Survey map of Bristol (sheet 264, solid and drift edition): a spread of browns and greys, tongues and folds and mattresses, pressings and contusions and bleeds, a bruised body, the injured ground beneath our feet.

The stone felt bad enough unpassed. At school, aged eleven, hiding at the out-field boundary, I stopped a six in my pubescent groin, winded by a well-struck cricket ball. Aged fifty-six, at home after hospital, I felt the same pain for three months. I knew, by then, that I was unlikely to pass the stone, but the thought alone made me curve tighter, more foetally – from a time before bone – into myself.

I got stones in my passway and all my roads seem dark as night.

Awaiting granulation by laser, I lived around a rocky shadow, peeing various bloody and earthy vintages with wincing trepidation, walking with difficulty, and, latterly, stooping in anguish as I stood. On good days, I felt like the Little Prince, drawn leaning nervously over his own planet; on bad ones, like Sisyphus wedded to his rock. The medical talk I longed for was of a divorce: the smashing of the globe to something gritty that might exit my body as gravel, or sand, or, better still, dust.

The Living Landscape of Britain gives the international standard measurements determining rock sizes – for 1952 at least: stones are 2 mm or more in diameter, coarse sand is 0.2–2 mm, fine sand is 0.02–0.2 mm, silt is 0.002–0.02 mm, and clay is less than 0.002 mm.

When I came round after my first operation, out of the nothing-bliss of anaesthesia, I had had a catheter fitted. The stent allowed out the stuff that the stone had blocked. As well as making my own rock, I had been sickly busy with finer and dirtier calculus. My catheter bag, taped to my thigh like a gunslinger's holster, filled with a bloody custard or what the nurses, who siphoned it off, called 'sludge'.

Laid low, on my bed, I read.

In Clarence Ellis's *The Pebbles on the Beach* (1954) there is a chapter titled 'The Birth, Life and Death of a Pebble':

> Pebble-hunting is a pleasant and health-giving hobby, whether pursued on the beach, the lake-side or the river bank, and all but those who are nearing the last stages of decrepitude can enjoy it.

Francis Ponge, among the great French phenomenological poets of the twentieth century, has a long prose poem called 'Le Galet' or 'The Pebble': 'a pebble is a stone at the precise moment when its life as a person, an individual, begins, I mean at the stage of speech.' The poem is, in part, about making art, but it is also an imagining of the death-in-life of the hard matter of our planet:

> Since the explosion of their colossal ancestor, and their trajectory across the heavens, beaten back without recourse, the rocks have fallen silent.

> Over-run and cracked by germination, like a man who has stopped shaving, hollowed out and filled with loose earth, no longer capable of reacting, not one of them utters a word

> Their faces, their bodies split. Naïveté comes to the wrinkles of experience and settles in. Roses perch on their grey laps and mumble their simple-minded diatribes against them. They let them. They, whose disastrous hail once cleared forests, whose time is for ever, reduced to stupor and resignation.

Gaston Bachelard, French phenomenologist-in-chief, writing about shells in *The Poetics of Space*, discusses the pre-Darwin evolutionary ideas of the eighteenth-century French naturalist, Jean-Baptiste Robinet. He believed that stones, especially fossils, were 'roughcasts' of body parts, with each organ having its 'own causality that has already been tried out during the long centuries when nature was teaching herself to make man.' Robinet's books are illustrated with fabulous engravings of penis-shaped and vulval stones, and others that imitate the ear, the eye, the hand, and the kidney. Robinet thinks of form 'from the inside out' Bachelard says.

In the summer of 1801, Coleridge often went walking in the Lake District. On June 18 he found a rest stop and a *bedrock*:

> A Hollow place in the Rock like a Coffin – a Sycamore Bush at the head, enough to give a shadow for my Face, & just at the Foot one tall Foxglove – exactly my own Length – there I lay & slept – It was quite soft.

Guy Davenport, essayist and novelist, was born in South Carolina in 1927. There, he ate mud. He writes about it in an essay in his book called *The Geography of the Imagination*:

> One of my great culinary moments was being taken as a tot to my black nurse's house to eat clay. 'What this child needs,' she had muttered one day while we were out, 'is a bait of clay.' Everybody in South Carolina knew that blacks, for reasons wunknown, fancied clay. Not until I came to read Toynbee's *A Study of History* years later did I learn that eating clay, or geophagy, is a prehistoric habit (it fills the stomach until you can bring down another aurochs) surviving only in West Africa and South Carolina.
>
> The eating took place in a bedroom, for the galvanised bucket of clay was kept under the bed, for the cool. It was blue clay from a creek, the consistency of slightly gritty ice cream. It lay smooth and delicious-looking in its pail of clear water. You scooped it out and ate it from your hand. The taste was wholesome, mineral and emphatic.

'I took advantage of being at the seaside to lay in a store of sucking-stones' – Molloy, in Samuel Beckett's novel of the same name, prefers pebbles over mud.

> I took a pebble from my pocket and sucked it. It was smooth, from having been sucked so long, by me, and beaten by the storm. A little pebble in your mouth, round and smooth, appeases, soothes, makes you forget your hunger, forget your thirst.

I lost weight. My ribs rose gaunt through my chest like a furrowed hillside. There seemed less of me than before; just skin and bone and the still-buried stone. Man's spirit in his bone-house dwells, wrote Gerard Manley Hopkins. Mine sank with my stone. I learned what rocky animals we are, we and the rest of the chordata, built around our cartilaginous skeletal rods. And, coming after that, just fossil selves or stony relics or dust and no more. After my first crisis, I didn't think that death would put in a claim right away, but the stone moved on me, and came to determine and define everything that I was. It dragged like an anchor. My thoughts weighed as it did. All my stories became one – a life beneath a lodestone, a stone in the heart of me, like the toad's crystalline jewel crowning its leathery head and piloting everything.

A kidney stone is made, most often, of calcium oxalate. The same salt is used in manufacturing ceramic glazes. Calcium and oxalate – some produced in the body, some found in foodstuffs – are very insoluble when mixed together in urine, and when concentrated in it, they crystallise. A seed-crystal forms and adheres to an internal surface of a kidney. There, in a renal cave, it grows and aggregates, drip by drip, rather like a stalagmite.

Our courtship had lasted for ages. I have been a stone-former for at least a decade and had long known of my *masonic* disposition. Small stones had been picked up before on one scan of my kidneys after a bloody urinary tract infection, but they did little otherwise to advertise themselves. I recognised the pain, knew its source when it woke me, but I hadn't known I'd been feeding a boulder for years.

Before a sea tide ebbs on a beach, a grazing limpet heads home…to its home scar. The shape of the bivalve's shell can grow to precisely match the contours of the rock where it fixes; the limpet marks the rock, the rock marks the limpet. Richard Pearce has been counting the same in North Cornwall ever since the oiling disaster that followed the sinking of the *Torrey Canyon* in 1967. Before I got ill, he had shown me Porthmear beach where there are, he has counted, one million home scars.

My wife, Claire, was born in Cape Town. She grew up in the shadow of Table Mountain and climbed its cliffs and gorges with her father and her friends. Exposed rock pressed on her life, early and deeply, a home-scar imprint such that her current sometime-stays in the apparently rockless flats of the fens around Cambridge feel like a de-boning exile.

She and I live sometimes there on the silt and the peat, as well as in Bristol, but sometimes also on the rocky peninsula that extends southwards from Table Mountain to become the Cape of Good Hope. Our village on the Atlantic shore, crouching beneath cliffs and various bergs, has attracted new-age rock workers. As I lay in wait for deliverance in Bristol, I followed the local news in Scarborough. A spotted eagle owl was picked up, apparently ill. Its finder dispensed two medicines. The bird was fed porridge and a healing crystal was hung around its neck. It was put overnight in a comfy box, but the next morning was found dead, flat on its face.

In my recuperation, I slowly walked a little of the Suffolk coast at Covehithe and Benacre. There were gulls feeding inland on the muddy pig fields, and there was the sea hungry at the shore all along the beach. The cliffs of sand are new, the water is at work, shouldering off hods of stuff on its tides, carrying flints and bones, gravels and house bricks down the North Sea. The beach is broken at Benacre and the reedy broad that was once there is now a brackish lagoon. The wood, at its fringe, is collapsing where the sea bites, and undermined trees, their ground taken from beneath them, have fallen towards the saltwater like woody skeletons.

The second leg of my walking-cure included a trip to the Great Rift, the opening of the earth that runs south from the Red Sea deep into southern Africa, like an epic ditch or a kind of anti-backbone. Lammergeiers are birds of the Rift walls and Ethiopian highlands and, on a previous visit near the rock churches of Lalibela, I'd watched the huge rusty vultures or ossifrage pick up livestock bones – vertebrae and femurs – from stony mountainsides, and drop them back onto the hard ground, shattering the osseous tissue for the softer marrow within. Their diet is more exclusively bone than any other bird. In the sierras of Spain, where the lammergeier is also known, it is called the *quebrantahuesos*, or bone-breaker.

I never saw my own stone, nor was anything other than unconscious when it was, first, approached and cordoned off, and then, later, detonated and collected. I imagine it white and round, its own planet; in fact it may well have been jagged and brown, a conglomerate of grits, more like the case of a caddisfly larva than Jupiter.

Wikipedia has a page on famous people who have had kidney stones. Samuel Pepys is the best-known sufferer – best-known, because he kept his stone in his mind as well as on his desk.

His started out in his bladder. He had lived under a succession of 'fits of stone' since he was a student at Cambridge. For years he was in pain and peeing blood. I know a little of this. For six weeks, my toilet splashed red every time I visited. I never got used to the colour or to the thought of all that wasted blood draining from me.

Surgery was a last resort in Pepys's time, but, aged twenty-five on March 26, 1658, he braved it. He was held down and tied to a chair or a table in the house of a friend. Tied – to keep him still, and to prevent him from running away. There was no anaesthesia.

Thomas Hollier, expert lithotomist, removed Pepys's stone. He worked fast. The extraction took less than a minute. Claire Tomalin's account of the surgery is terrifyingly gripping:

> First he inserted a thin silver instrument, the itinerarium, through the penis into the bladder to help position the stone. Then he made the incision, about three inches long and a finger's breadth from the line running between scrotum and anus, and into the neck of the bladder, or just below it. The patient's face was sponged as the incision was made. The stone was sought, found and grasped with pincers; the more speedily it could be got out the better. Once out, the wound was not stitched – it was thought best to let it drain and cicatrize itself – but simply washed and covered with a dressing, or even kept open at first with a small roll of soft cloth known as a tent, dipped in egg white. A plaster of egg yolk, rose vinegar and anointing oils was then applied.

The stone rolled out intact, the size of a tennis ball. Real-tennis, as it was then, used smaller balls than Wimbledon, but Pepys's stone was still about 50 millimetres across. If both his and mine were spherical, and if size is taken as volume, then his was 578.7 times as big as mine. He was up and walking two weeks after he was cut.

Pepys marked his operation day for many years. He was proud of his stone, had special dinners in commemoration, and had his prize set in a wooden case that cost him twenty-four shillings. On the fourth anniversary in 1662 ('the Lord's name be praised for it'), he had a lunch for three guests: 'a brace of stewed carps, six roasted chickens, a jowl of salmon, hot, for the first course; a tanzy [pudding] and two neats' tongues [ox or cow], and cheese, the second'. In his diary for June 1669, John Evelyn records getting Pepys to show his stone ('as big as a tenis-ball') to Evelyn's similarly afflicted brother, 'to encourage his resolution to go through with the operation'.

In 1669, the last twelve months of his diary, Pepys recalled the day of his surgery but forgot the year. When he died, aged seventy, in 1703, he had survived forty-five years since he was cut. Some have speculated that he was also given an accidental vasectomy at the same time. He never fathered a child. An autopsy revealed that the old malady was still at work: the original wound had broken open and Pepys had a gangrenous bladder. There were also seven stones in his left kidney.

Almost three months to the day after my first admission to Southmead hospital, I went back. Mr Timoney marked me up with his black pen. I was talking about *The Archers*, and then I was waking in a nappy and being offered a drink of water. In between, the surgeon had taken a laser and a camera and what he called a 'basket' on a brief trip, via my penis, inside me. He had been able to collect most of what he blasted. Blood spotted my nappy but, even climbing out of the fog of anaesthesia, I felt better than I had in months. I could stand without aching and my eyes met further horizons than I had seen for weeks. The pain, in fact, got worse, but only for two days as the last of the shattered stone left me, dragging a train of coarse sand, and I yelped and had to be held at the shoulders by Claire as I stood at the toilet. After that, I ate ice cream and fattened myself, and stretched flabbily outwards, never so soft and rockless, never so happy not to know my insides.

Mr Timoney wrote to me. The stone 'reserved at the time of your ureteroscopy' was an ordinary calcium oxalate one. This type, he continued, 'is likely to recur within eight years unless you increase your fluid intake by two litres per twenty-four hours, avoid added salt and avoid weight gain…'

I fill my glass from the tap. And then again.

Meteorites
ABOVE AND BEYOND
Diane Johnson

When I started to collect meteorites as a teenager I had no idea that I would end up working on them. By the time I was sixteen I had as many as the British Museum in 1802, when it launched its meteorite collection with a princely three specimens. I was fascinated by the night sky, and have always felt a deep connection with meteorites. They are an astronomy I can behold. When near them, the hairs prickle on the back of my neck.

One of my earliest meteorites was a slice of a *pallasite*, called Brenham, named after where it was found: Brenham, Kansas, USA. Big and rounded, bright with orange, brown and green olivine crystals twinkling like disco lights. It is embedded within a nickel-rich iron metal which reflects light with a silvery metallic sheen and darts around the edges like a bolt of lightning. Pallasites rarely fail to impress and are probably what most people imagine an object from space should look like.

In movies, all meteorites blaze across the sky and slam into the Earth with a deafening boom, leaving a vast crater around them. Such a strike is famously attributed to the extinction of the dinosaurs 66 million years ago, pushing evolution of life on Earth into a different direction. The Chicxulub crater in Mexico is believed to have been an asteroid strike: a very large rocky body in space that made a seven-mile-wide impact on Earth. Compare the apocalyptic Technicolour Hollywood vision of the end of the dinosaurs with the Tunguska meteorite explosion of 1908, which flattened 2,000 square kilometres of Siberian taiga, felling outwards in a radial pattern some 80 million trees. Scientists remain puzzled as to what actually happened. Some believe that the meteor exploded in mid-air, producing a shock wave that hit the ground and left no crater at all, nor indeed much, if any, hard evidence of extraterrestrial meteorite material.

Whatever happened at Tunguska, most meteorites are actually small, so very small indeed that they're dust. Conservative estimates suggest that the Earth gains mass from meteorites by approximately 40,000 tonnes per year, and most of this is meteorite dust. The room you are in right now is very likely to contain a grain of dust from space, the remnant of a shooting star that burnt up in Earth's atmosphere. The astronomer Carl Sagan was right: we and our households are made of stardust.

There are three basic types of meteorites defined by their compositions: stones, irons and stony-irons. Each type has undergone its own particular formation processes, defined by its complicated history, and its specific chemical and structural traits. These meteorite types ultimately originate from the planetary formation processes that shaped the solar system into what we see today. Studying meteorites can help us understand how planets form: clues are hidden in their microscopic, mineral structures, providing tiny but precise chemical traces of the birth and evolution of the solar system.

If we go back 4.6 billion years, when Earth was created, the solar system was no more than a swirling cloud of gas and dust. Gradually, gravity pulled the cloud together, and at its centre was an embryonic version of the Sun, with a disc of material surrounding it. When its density reached a critical level, fusion reactions of hydrogen, the Sun's most abundant ingredient, started to produce energy as a natural giant nuclear reactor. This represented the birth of the Sun, which, producing its own energy, emitted radiation including visible light, and an ionic wind that pushed away nearby debris in the solar disc. A variety of theories exist for the exact formation process of planets, but all involve condensation, cooling and consolidation processes, together producing small solid particles within the solar disc, gravity forever trying to pull them together, and gradually building up rocky planetary bodies. These very early solid structures, millimetres or less in size, are typically still visible in some of the more primitive stony meteorites, called *chondrites*. These small particles gradually built up to form asteroids.

At times, the early solar system was a violent place, with collisions between these early asteroids. Sometimes they would fragment, but often the energy involved would be transferred as heat and cause melting and shock to the rocks. This can also be seen in some of the stony meteorites that fall to earth, with angular shards of distinctly different textures and dark melt veins, where molten rock has pushed through fractures.

From prehistoric cultures to modern societies, people have always interacted with meteorites. The earliest recorded European meteorite fall portrayed in a painting was by the young Albrecht Dürer, in around 1492, and depicts the fireball of the Ensisheim meteorite in Alsace, eastern France. There, villagers witnessed a 127-kilogram meteorite fall from the sky into a field of wheat. When Emperor Maximilian I received a report of this event, he declared it an omen of divine protection against invasion and ordered it to be chained to the wall in a local church. A large part of it is still on display in Ensisheim today.

An early recorded British meteorite fall was in Yorkshire. The 'Wold Cottage meteorite' that fell into a field in 1795 was witnessed by local farm workers, who gave sworn statements about the incident. When British maritime explorers encountered a tribe of Inuits in north-western Greenland in 1818, they were astounded to find that they had knife blades, harpoon points and engraving tools made of meteoric iron, derived from what's called the 'Cape York meteorite' which was split into pieces and worked into functional objects without the use of heat. Part of this large meteorite fall was a 20-tonne iron meteorite known as Agpalilik ('the man') discovered in Northern Greenland in 1963, and which is now on display in the Geological Museum in Copenhagen. It is the largest single iron crystal that is known.

Meteorites are also found at archaeological sites across the globe, both in their natural form and worked into shapes. The earliest-known examples of iron in Egypt were excavated in 1911 at the Gerzeh cemetery, about forty miles south of Cairo. Two grave pits were found to contain beads of iron and date from prehistoric times, around 3,000 years before the earliest evidence of large-scale iron smelting. When I had the opportunity to examine one of these beads, I discovered a crystallographic pattern known as Widmanstätten, which is a unique characteristic of certain types of iron meteorites. If you cut, polish and lightly etch such an iron meteorite, this pattern can be seen with the naked eye as interweaving parallel and reflective bands.

The Gerzeh iron beads are unique, made of 4.5 billion-year-old iron that was forged inside the core of a protoplanet, which in turn was found on Earth and purposefully worked into beads that were ultimately worn by an important prehistoric man in his grave. The Gerzeh iron meteorite wasn't like any meteorite I've ever seen before, a tubular shape covered in rust and sand grains. At first glance this rarity didn't look so very special – you could easily walk past it without giving it a second glance. But with the bead placed in an electron microscope I could see areas of preserved metal with meteorite chemistry. There were tell-tale distortions of the metal structure indicating where the metal had been beaten to form the bead, and I could also see remnants of the fibres of thread used to string the beads around their owner's neck. More scientific analysis is needed, but it is clear that iron was a very special material in ancient Egypt. It had a strong association with the sky, and from the early nineteenth Dynasty onwards, approximately 1,300 BC, the ancient Egyptian hieroglyphic term meaning 'iron' literally translates as 'iron from the sky'.

Among the many funerary objects in the tomb of Tutankhamun, nineteen nickel-rich iron objects were discovered, including a set of blades of a design very similar to those used in the 'Opening of the Mouth' ceremony – a ritual performed to reanimate the deceased, allowing them to take food and offerings into the afterlife. Also in the tomb of Tutankhamun, wrapped with his mummy, was an iron dagger blade and golden bracelet with an iron eye of Horus attached to it, symbolising protection and healing. There was the miniature headrest, too, made from iron, that was found directly behind Tutankhamun's head, inside the golden death mask. Such model headrests were considered to be symbolically linked to the protection of the dead and resurrection, the shiny reflective iron possibly representing a reflection of the real world of the living into the afterlife of the deceased.

The universe is 13.8 billion years old and so big that we can't physically observe it all from Earth, as the light emitted has so far to travel. When the main formation had taken place, gathering the asteroids into significant-sized planetary bodies, or *protoplanets*, their evolution remained incomplete. A process known as 'planetary differentiation' would still take place, whereby heavy elements such as metals like iron and nickel were being pulled to the centre of the protoplanet, gravity forming internal structures of a metal iron-nickel core, with a rocky mantle layer sandwiched between the surface crust. If these protoplanets suffered a massive impact they could fragment again, producing melted, recrystallised materials, further altered by the early solar system's formation processes.

In meteorites we have a range of samples from these types of early evolving planetary bodies in the solar system. In addition to samples from Mars and the Moon, these meteorites escaped from their parent bodies by impact, events that ultimately brought them into Earth-orbit, allowing them to fall. Meteorites, therefore, are snapshots of space and time, representing the solar system through its existence over the last 4,600 million years.

The gaseous planets in the solar system have also played a role in the formation of the rocky planets. A giant gaseous planet, such as Jupiter, can be considered to be a failed star which never quite achieved a sufficient density of hydrogen to produce energy by fusion (like the Sun). However, its large gravitational presence prevented a further rocky planet from forming between it and Mars: the rocky debris within this orbit could not pull itself into a single body, and was effectively caught in a tug of war between Jupiter and the Sun. This is why today we have an asteroid belt between Mars and Jupiter. And it is from this asteroid belt that we receive most of the meteorites found on Earth. A jumbled collection of left-over pieces of the early solar system, denied by gravity to form into a planet.

Temperature variation through the solar system also influenced its material compositions. The inner solar system was hotter than the outer parts, primarily because of the Sun, so any delicate volatile matter such as water or organic molecules would have been ionised, broken down and swept away by the ions being emitted by the Sun. But the outer solar system was colder, where we can still see remnants of the very early delicate organics and water in the form of comets.

Each time a comet passes through the inner solar system close to the Sun, some of its surface will heat up, melting part of its ice, forming a vapour which will escape, vented out into space. The comet landscape can change drastically, perhaps losing tens of metres' depth from its surface with each pass around the Sun. Chunks of the rocky materials, enriched with organic molecules mixed within its icy body, can then also separate away from the comet, leaving a path of debris in the comet's orbit. When Earth crosses this orbit, gravity attracts the cometary fragments to enter Earth's atmosphere. The material surviving entry to reach the ground as meteorites are examples of this delicate, early- and low-temperature solar-system material. These types of meteorites are one of the stony meteorites known as *carbonaceous chondrites*. The organic molecules they contain can be very complex and similar to the organic molecular building blocks that all living creatures are made from. Although impressive to know what they are made of, to the naked eye they look very modest, dark and generally only have the strength of chalk, but can be so rich in organics that when found soon after they land on Earth are described as having a pungent, creosote smell.

Meteorites have long cemented ideas that link human origins with the heavens and ideas of divine creation. Such a stone lies at the heart of Mecca. Set into the south-eastern corner of the Kaaba, the cubic granite structure at the centre of the Grand Mosque, and in the direction of which, Muslims the world over pray five times a day, is what's called the Black Stone, the al-Hajar al-Aswad. Highly polished by the touch and kisses of millions of pilgrims over hundreds of years, the stone has long been described as a meteorite. It is said that it was placed there by Mohammed. Tradition holds that the Black Stone figured in the story of Abraham, the significant foundational figure of the three monotheistic faiths of Judaism, Islam and Christianity. The Black Stone is also said to have served as an altar for Adam and Eve, representing the first temple on earth. Perhaps it is fitting that what has long been considered to be a meteorite should be the cornerstone of a place where the mundane intersects with the heavenly.

Acknowledgements

This book began life as talks for BBC Radio 3's late-night Essay series. Thank you to Matthew Dodd, head of the network's Speech Programmes, for having encouraged them through four series, which are still available online. And thank you to Adrian Cooper of Little Toller for giving the radio talks an afterlife in this book. I hope that the immediacy of pieces written specifically for the voice is still conveyed, and that the writer's distinctive voice lifts off the page.

As much as possible, the radio essays were all recorded outdoors, taking the listener out into the landscapes that are evoked, away from the green baize and polite hush of the radio studio. Better the dash of the wind against the mic, and the crunch of stone underfoot. This led to memorable moments, for example, hunkering down out of the wind at the base of the enormous sand dunes north of Aberdeen while Esther Woolfson linked the North Sea's hydrocarbon industries with the Granite City nearby. I remember recording along Stanage Edge in the Peak District with the poet and climber Helen Mort as she described the rub of the millstone grit, then both of us gawping as a hang glider flew low overhead.

The collection includes five pieces that offer rocky takes on different northern latitudes, and were commissioned for Radio 3's Northern Lights season. Thanks to Tim Dee, Neil Ansell and Diane Johnson for agreeing to add their pieces to those already broadcast by the BBC, and to Alan Garner and Curtis Brown for permission to publish 'Flint', a spellbinding piece about the sparks of fire, the arrowheads and hand axes that enabled human evolution. Thanks also to Rodney Harris, whose incredbile strata map of England and Wales is inspirted by William Smith's 1815 *Map of the British Isles*, and uses ground up rock samples from each area to create its unique map of the true colours of strata.

M. S.
Bristol, 2018

Contributors

Neil Ansell is the author of three books: *Deep Country: Five Years in the Welsh Hills*, *Deer Island* and *The Last Wilderness: A Journey into Silence*. He spent many years working his way around the world, but is currently settled on chalk by the sea with his two daughters.

John Burnside was born in Fife, and grew up in Corby, Northamptonshire. He spent many years as a computer systems designer until he became a writer in 1996. His 2012 poetry collection *Black Cat Bone* won the T. S. Eliot Prize and Forward Prize. He has published nine books of fiction, three memoirs and, more recently, the novella *Havergey* and a book on Henry Miller. He also teaches at the University of St Andrews.

Linda Cracknell lives among the hills in Highland Perthshire. She has had several dramas broadcast on BBC Radio 4 and has published two collections of short stories and a novel, *Call of the Undertow*. A committed walker, her collection *Doubling Back: Ten Paths Trodden in Memory* was published in 2014 and was a Radio 4 Book of the Week. She is currently a Royal Literary Fund fellow at the University of Stirling.

Gillian Clarke was the National Poet of Wales 2008–16, and is President of Tŷ Newydd, the Welsh Writers' Centre. She was awarded the Queen's Gold Medal for Poetry 2010, the Wilfred Owen Poetry Award 2012 and the Hay Festival Poetry Medal 2016. Picador published *Selected Poems* in 2016. Her latest collection, *Zoology*, was published by Carcanet in 2017.

Sue Clifford worked as a landscape planner in Edinburgh and as a lecturer in land planning and environmental activism. She was on the Board of Directors of the fledgling Friends of the Earth from the early 1970s into the 80s, and in 1982 she co-founded the arts and environmental charity Common Ground with Angela King and Roger

Deakin. She has also written extensively for Common Ground, notably, with Angela King, *England in Particular*.

Tim Dee is author of *Landfill*, a book about gulls and people. He has also written *The Running Sky* and *Four Fields* and edited *The Poetry of Birds* (with Simon Armitage) and *Ground Work*. He was a BBC radio producer for twenty-eight years.

Paul Evans is a nature writer and senior lecturer in creative writing at Manchester Metropolitan University. He is best known as a contributor of Country Diaries for *The Guardian* and as a writer and presenter of natural history documentaries, radio poems and docu-dramas on BBC Radio 4. His books include *Herbaceous*, *Field Notes from the Edge* and *How To See Nature*. He lives in Much Wenlock, Shropshire, with his family.

Rose Ferraby is an archaeologist, artist and cultural geologist. She co-directs the Aldborough Roman Town Project in North Yorkshire and has dug deeper to look at the cultural geologies of the Jurassic Coast. Rose published *Stonework* with Mark Edmonds and was winner of the Michael Marks Award for Poetry Illustration in 2017 for *The Tender Map* by Melanie Challenger.

Alan Garner was born in Cheshire and his childhood was spent in Alderley Edge, where his family has lived for more than four hundred years. He was awarded the OBE in 2001 for his services to literature. Philip Pullman has described Alan, whose novels include *Owl Service* and *Red Shift*, as being 'indisputably the great originator, the most important British writer of fantasy since Tolkien.' His memoir *Where Shall We Run To?* was published in 2018.

Alyson Hallett's poetry pamphlet, *Toots*, was shortlisted for the Michael Marks and Callum MacDonald Memorial Awards. She has curated the international poetry-as-public-art project, The Migration Habits of Stones, for the past eighteen years. She has also published two full volumes of poetry and several artist's books, short stories, an afternoon play and an audio-diary for BBC Radio 4. She lives in Bath.

Fiona Hamilton's poetry includes *Bite Sized*, *Project Boast* and *Fractures*. The last involved responding to buildings and environments in collaboration with artists and local inhabitants, including insects and sheep. She is tutor and research adviser at Metanoia Institute and Orchard Foundation, where her work includes enhancing understanding of mental health issues using creative arts.

Diane Johnson is a research fellow at the Camborne School of Mines, University of Exeter, and an honorary research associate with the Open University, School of Physical Sciences. She applies advanced technology to solve complex analytical issues in the fields of planetary science and archaeology. With special interests in iron meteorites and cultural aspects of meteorites, she is frequently involved in research exploring the use and perception of meteorite iron by ancient Egyptians.

Daniel Kalder was born and raised in Fife. In 1997, he moved to Russia and spent the better part of the next decade working, living and travelling in and around the former Soviet Union. This experience led to two works of reportage, *Lost Cosmonaut* and *Strange Telescopes*, and which culminated with the publication of *Dictator Literature*. He lives in Austin, Texas.

Sara Maitland's first novel, *Daughter of Jerusalem*, won the Somerset Maugham Award in 1979 and since then she has been a writer of novels, short stories and non-fiction. More recently she published *A Book of Silence* and *Gossip from the Forest* and is working on a book about 'the uncanny' in British landscapes for Little Toller. She has two grown-up children and lives alone on a high moor in Galloway.

Jason Mark is the author of *Satellites in the High Country: Searching for the Wild in the Age of Man* and is the editor-in-chief of *SIERRA*, the national magazine of the Sierra Club. His writings on the environment have appeared in *The New York Times*, *Los Angeles Times*, *The Nation*, and *The Atlantic*, among many other publications. He lives in Oakland, California.

Helen Mort has published two poetry collections, *Division Street* and *No Map Could Show Them*. Her first novel, *Black Car Burning*, is forthcoming and her latest publication is *The Singing Glacier*, a cycle of poems inspired by the glaciers of East Greenland.

Gina Moseley is a geologist at the University of Innsbruck, Austria, where she specialises in using cave-based deposits to study past climate change. Her research expeditions have taken her all over the world, from the Tropics to the Arctic, and her work has won many awards.

Sarah Moss is the author of six novels, three shortlisted for the Wellcome Book Prize, and a memoir of her year in Iceland, *Names for the Sea*, shortlisted for the Royal Society of Literature Ondaatje Prize. Her latest book, *Ghost Wall*, is set in the shadow of Hadrian's Wall. She is Professor of Creative Writing and Director of the Warwick Writing Programme at the University of Warwick.

Peter Randall-Page has an international reputation for his sculpture, drawings and prints. He has undertaken numerous large-scale commissions and his work is held widely in public and private collections throughout the world. He has been awarded an Honorary Doctorate from several universities and in June 2015 was elected as a Royal Academician.

Ronald Turnbull is an outdoor writer and photographer who has published walking guidebooks to several areas in Scotland, including the Cairngorms and the Lomond-Trossach National Park. Ronald lives on the Permian sandstone in Scotland's Southern Uplands.

Sara Wheeler's books include the international bestsellers *Terra Incognita: Travels in Antarctica, Magnetic North: Notes from the Arctic Circle* and *O My America!* She has published two biographies of travellers: *Cherry: A Life of Apsley Cherry-Garrard* and *Too Close to the Sun: The Life and Times of Denys Finch Hatton.* She lives in London.

Esther Woolfson is the author of *Corvus* and *Field Notes from a Hidden City*, which was shortlisted for the Royal Society of Literature Ondaatje Prize. An award-winning short-story writer, she has been Artist in Residence at Aberdeen Centre for Environmental Sustainability and Writer in Residence at Hexham Book Festival. She is an Honorary Fellow in the Department of Anthropology at Aberdeen University.

Little Toller Books

We publish old and new writing attuned to nature and the landscape, working with a wide range of the very best writers and artists. We pride ourselves on publishing affordable books of the highest quality. If you have enjoyed this book, you will also like exploring our other titles.

Anthology
ARBOREAL *Edited by Adrian Cooper*
CORNERSTONES *Edited by Mark Smalley*

Field Notes
MY HOME IS THE SKY: THE LIFE OF J. A. BAKER *Hetty Saunders*
DEER ISLAND *Neil Ansell*
ORISON FOR A CURLEW *Horatio Clare*
LOVE, MADNESS, FISHING *Dexter Petley*
WATER AND SKY *Neil Sentance*
THE TREE *John Fowles*

Monographs
HERBACEOUS *Paul Evans*
ON SILBURY HILL *Adam Thorpe*
SPIRITS OF PLACE *Sara Maitland*
THE ASH TREE *Oliver Rackham*
MERMAIDS *Sophia Kingshill*
SHARKS *Martha Sprackland*
BLACK APPLES OF GOWER *Iain Sinclair*
BEYOND THE FELL WALL *Richard Skelton*
LIMESTONE COUNTRY *Fiona Sampson*
HAVERGEY *John Burnside*
SNOW *Marcus Sedgwick*
LANDFILL *Tim Dee*

Nature Classics Library
THROUGH THE WOODS *H. E. Bates*
MEN AND THE FIELDS *Adrian Bell*
THE MIRROR OF THE SEA *Joseph Conrad*
ISLAND YEARS, ISLAND FARM *Frank Fraser Darling*
THE MAKING OF THE ENGLISH LANDSCAPE *W. G. Hoskins*
BROTHER TO THE OX *Fred Kitchen*
FOUR HEDGES *Clare Leighton*
DREAM ISLAND *R. M. Lockley*
THE UNOFFICIAL COUNTRYSIDE *Richard Mabey*
RING OF BRIGHT WATER *Gavin Maxwell*
EARTH MEMORIES *Llewelyn Powys*
IN PURSUIT OF SPRING *Edward Thomas*
THE NATURAL HISTORY OF SELBORNE *Gilbert White*

Little Toller Books
Lower Dairy, Toller Fratrum, Dorset
W. littletoller.co.uk **E.** books@littletoller.co.uk